MW01710020

WHAT IT IS

In making a picture the artist uses line, tone and color to create shapes. The position in relation to the borders, the size, the direction, their values in tone, color or texture are the means by which the artist designs his pictures. This designing, organizing or structuring a picture is composition. The words composition, design, organization, and structure will be used interchangeably throughout this book.

WHAT IT DOES

The organization of a picture performs many functions. It guides and directs the observer's eye, controls the speed of this movement and serves to direct the eye to the artist's choice of climax. It can help to communicate violence, stability, beauty, or ugliness. It can arouse, intensify or soothe emotional reactions.

The role that composition plays in picture making is demonstrated in the analyses, where recognizable subject matter has been removed and the basic design structure remains.

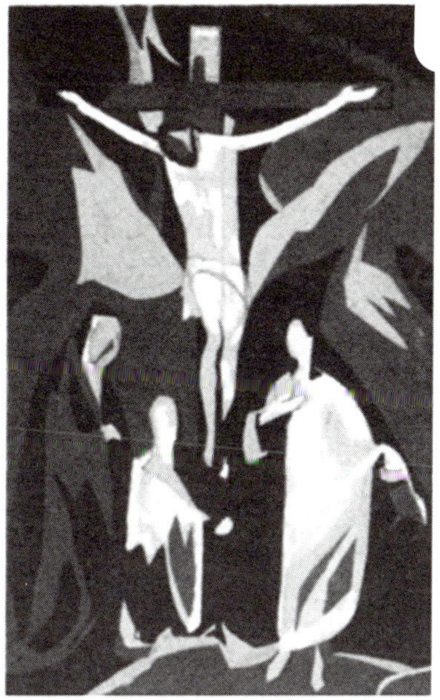

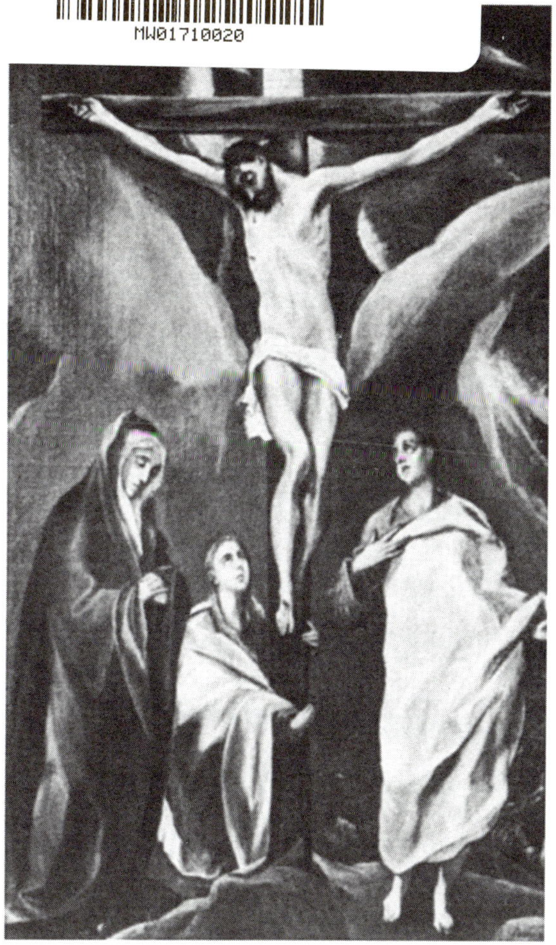

EL GRECO.
Christ on the Cross with the two Maries and Saint John.
Athens Picture Gallery.

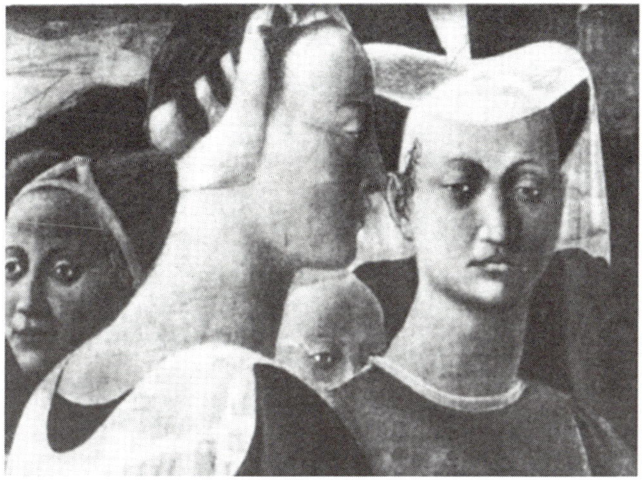

PIERRO DELLA FRANCESCA.
Detail.

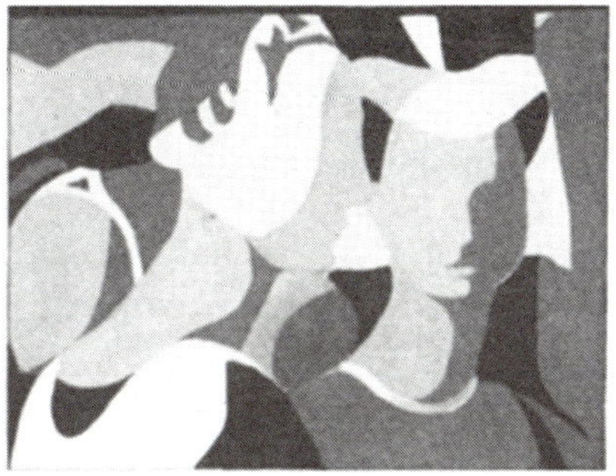

INTRODUCTION

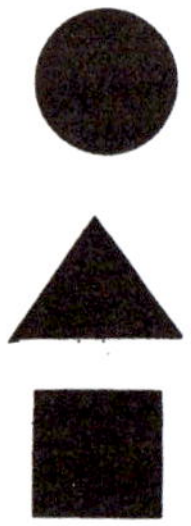

SHAPES IN NATURE

When the artist looks at nature and selects the material for his picture, he is frequently lost in the complexity of the elements. Whether he is academically realistic or semi-abstract, it is necessary for him to reduce the images to controllable simplicity. Confusing detail must be eliminated at this time.

Although all nature—man, mountain, leaf, and tree—is seemingly infinite in the complexity of its structures, all shapes in nature can be reduced to *the square, the circle and the triangle*. It is easier for the artist to compose his picture if he thinks in terms of these elementary shapes. After the picture is solidly designed, he can then add such details as he desires.

Sketch.

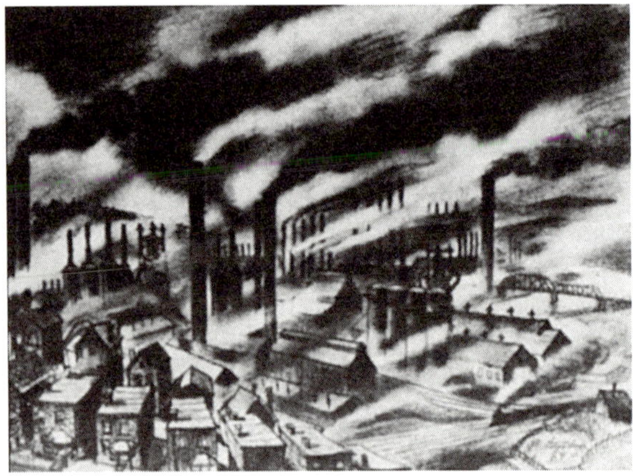

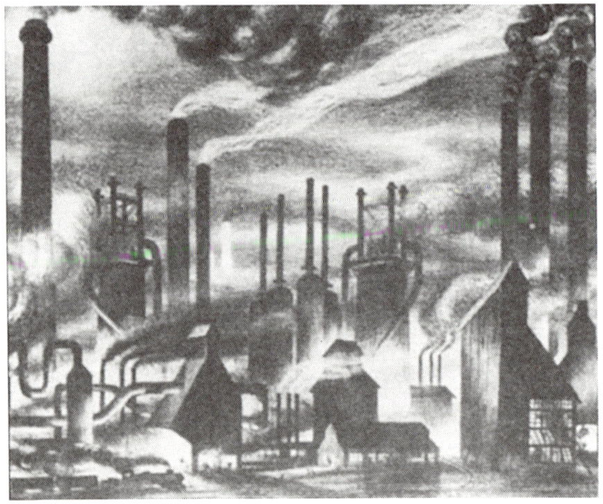

HARRY STERNBERG.
Bethlehem Steel.
Collection of the Artist.

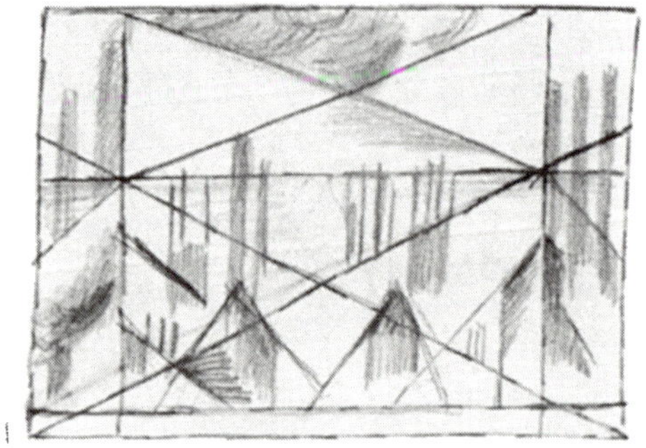

Structural Design.

Analysis.

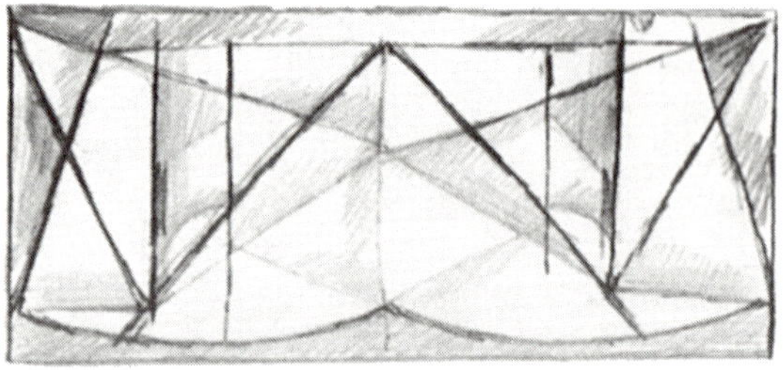

PICASSO.
Guernica.
Collection of the Artist.
Courtesy of The Museum of Modern Art.

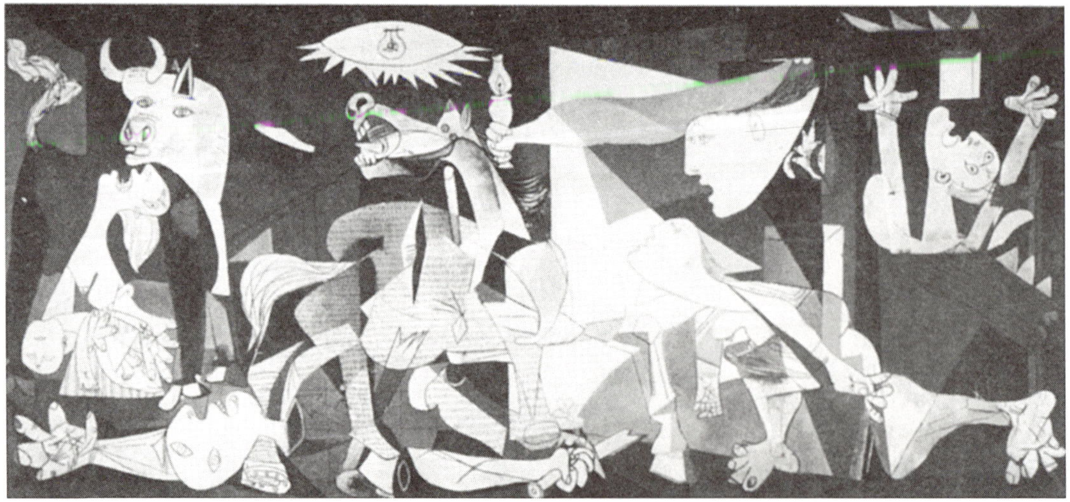

Composition

The Anatomy of Picture Making

HARRY STERNBERG

DOVER PUBLICATIONS, INC.
Mineola, New York

Bibliographical Note

This Dover edition, first published in 2008, is a republication of the work originally published in 1958 by Pitman Publishing Corp., New York.

Library of Congress Cataloging-in-Publication Data

Sternberg, Harry, 1904–2001.
Composition : the anatomy of picture making / Harry Sternberg.
p. cm.
"This Dover edition, first published in 2008, is a republication of the work originally published in 1958 by Pitman Publishing Corp., New York."
ISBN-13: 978-0-486-46595-1
ISBN-10: 0-486-46595-0
1. Compostion (Art). 2. Painting—Technique. I. Title.

ND1475.S74 2008
750.1'8—dc22

2007049439

Manufactured in the United States of America
Dover Publications, Inc., 31 East 2nd Street, Mineola, N.Y. 11501

INTRODUCTION

THE ARTIST LOOKS AT NATURE

Some artists still go hunting for compositions, armed with a cardboard viewer or "composition finder." Such artists peer through the slot in their viewers, seeking an arrangement in nature that fits satisfactorily into the opening. When they find it, they proceed to copy what they see.

The history of art demonstrates that artists, in their never-ending search for new and more personal ways of creating, continually revaluate all aspects of the creative act. They are constantly searching for freedom from the limitations imposed upon them by the latest academic tradition.

The contemporary artists recognized that they were coming into competition with the camera. Attempts to match technical facility against the mechanical effectiveness of the camera could only result in frustration.

One dramatic step that was taken by artists was literally and symbolically to throw away their view finders. Unhampered by the limitations of the view finder, they attained freedom in relation to their subjects. They could choose elements from different locations and arrange them in one picture to suit their particular esthetic and expressive needs. They could eliminate, emphasize and change the scale of the elements in their compositions. They found that not only could they design better, but that they could communicate better.

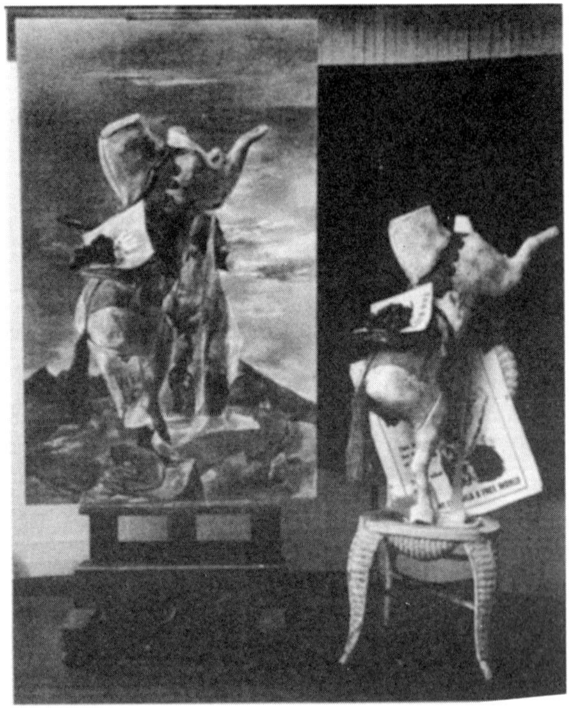

STUART DAVIS.
Summer Landscape.
Collection Museum of Modern Art.

Photograph of the Scene of Summer Landscape.
Photo Courtesy of Museum of Modern Art.

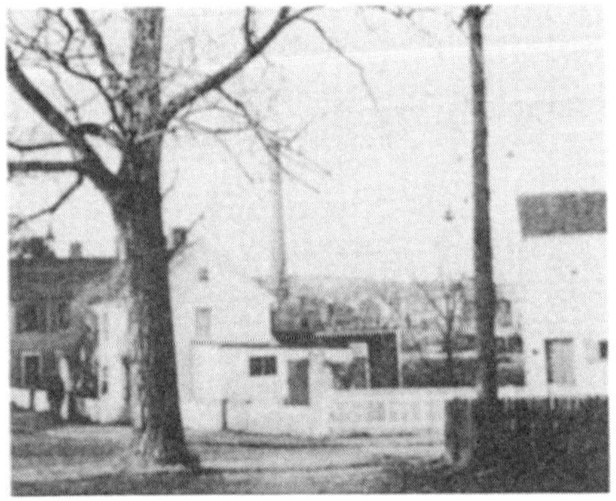

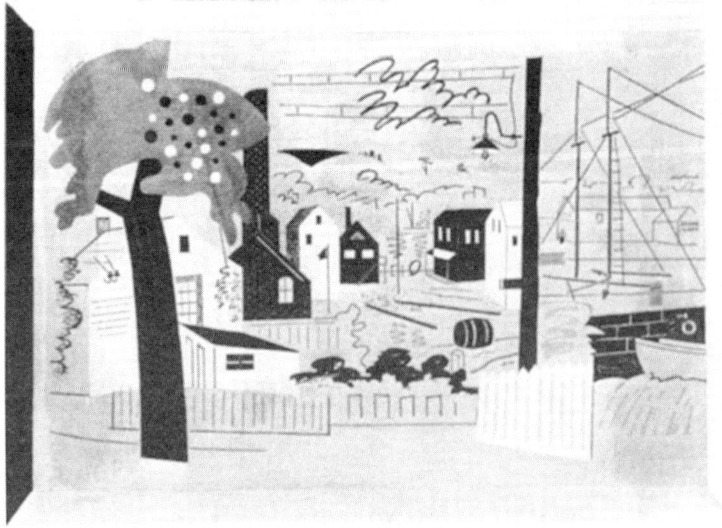

HOW WE SEE

How we see is a process so intricately involved that the act is as yet only partially understood. The mechanism of the eye has been anatomically dissected, but its function in relation to the brain is still unknown. We can only say that, through some combination of physiological and psychological factors, plus experience and learning, we see.

For our purpose in this book we shall concern ourselves only with the concept that experience and learning are important parts of seeing. Since every human being has a different set of experiences, *each sees differently.*

It is of interest to note that in the thousands of years of painting history there have been few and relatively brief periods in which artists concerned themselves with exact reproduction of nature. The artist has always seen nature *interpretatively.* Eastern artists changed the scale of their subjects according to their importance. Byzantine artists used flat design and the reverse of the perspective that we use. Distortion is common to all periods of art.

If we can remember that the way we see is the way we have been taught and trained to see, and if we recognize that new learning can teach us to see in new ways, we shall avoid bigoted attitudes.

KIYOMASU I.
Hanjuro in a Woman's Role.
Philadelphia Museum of Art.

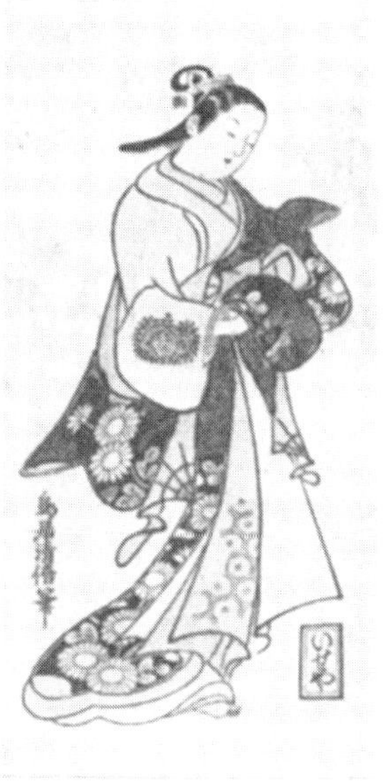

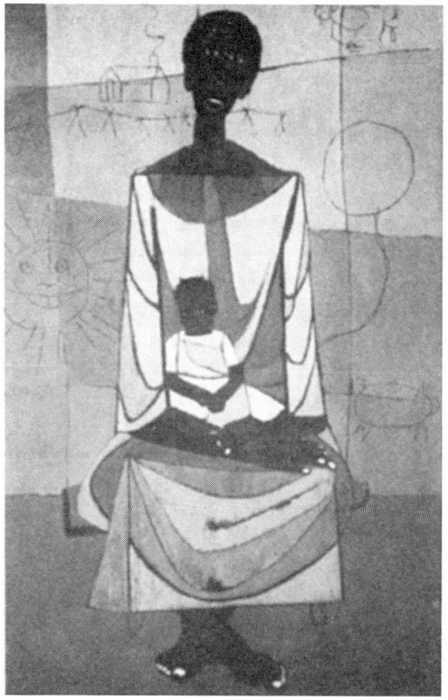

GWATHMEY.
Lullaby.
Collection of Mr. & Mrs. Robert Riley.
Photo Courtesy of ACA Gallery.

PICASSO.
Lithograph Portrait.

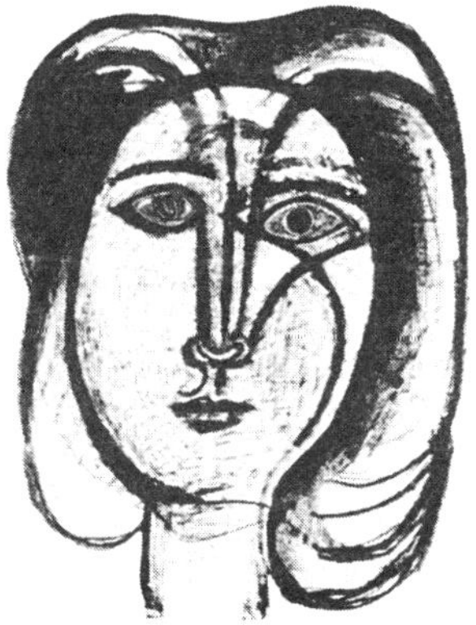

VAN DER WEYDEN.
Portrait of a Woman.
Kaiser Friedrich Museum.

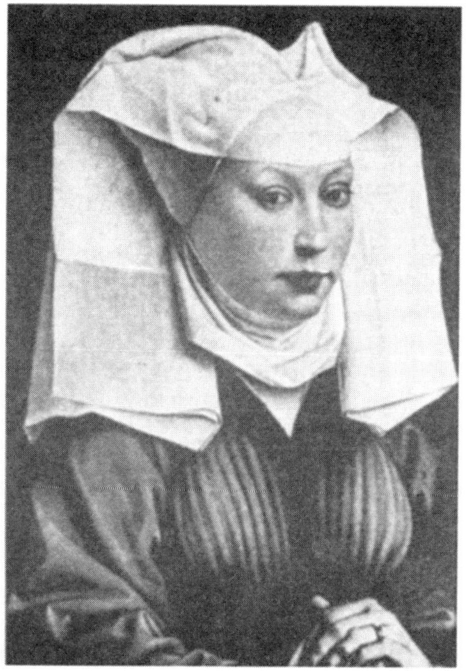

THE PICTURE BORDER

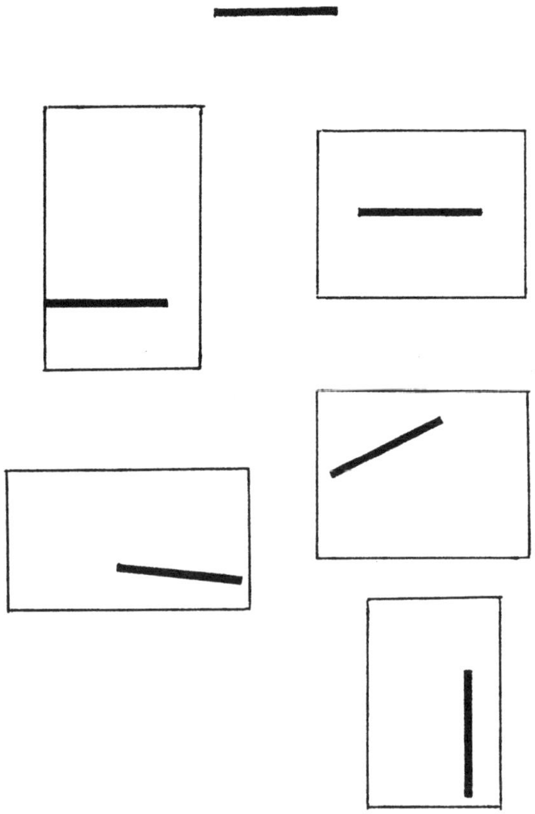

To begin a picture it is necessary first to establish the area in which the picture will be made by drawing the enclosing border. This picture border is frequently referred to as the picture frame, or the frame of reference. The vertical and horizontal lines of the border make a frame of reference for measuring the position and the activity of the elements in the picture.

Many artists begin a picture by drawing the subject and then attempting to enclose it with a border. This inevitably leads to compositional difficulties. It can be likened to the builder who erects the walls for his building and then attempts to place a foundation under them.

This principle of design is demonstrated by using a black square. Note that the square has no pictorial significance until it is related to a border. Only then can its activity and nature be understood, for the square changes into a triangle in a different frame relationship.

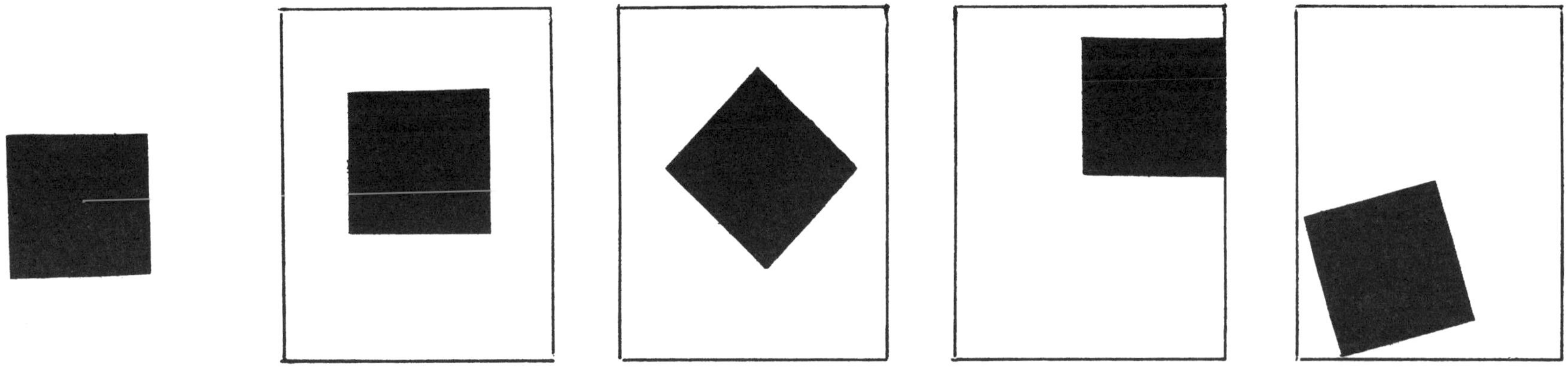

One photograph of the author was taken. By using an enlarger, the relationship of the figure to the border was changed in each of the four pictures.

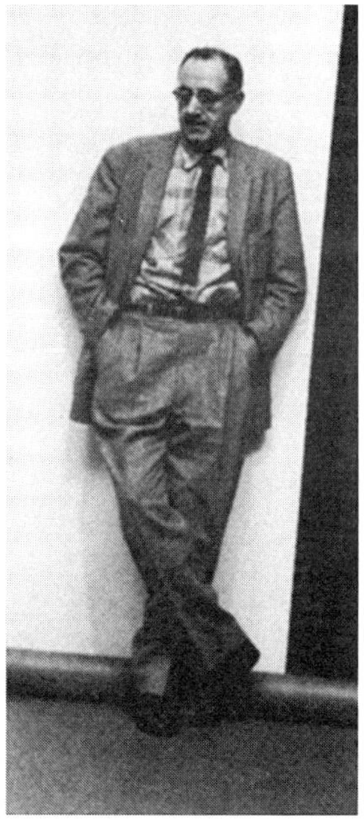

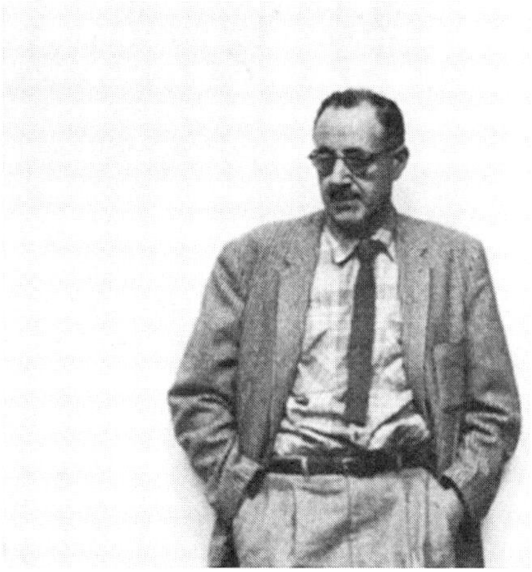

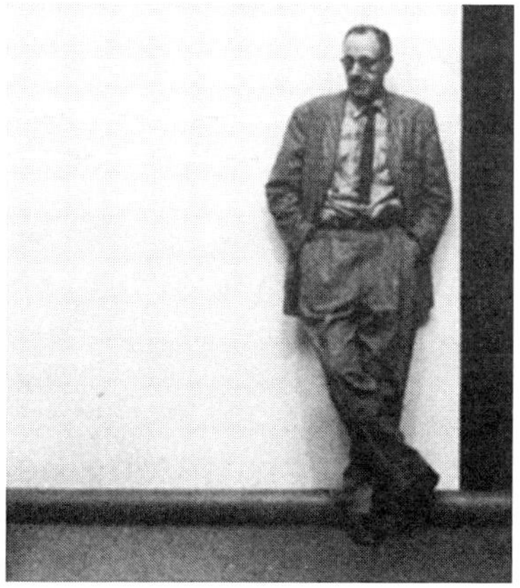

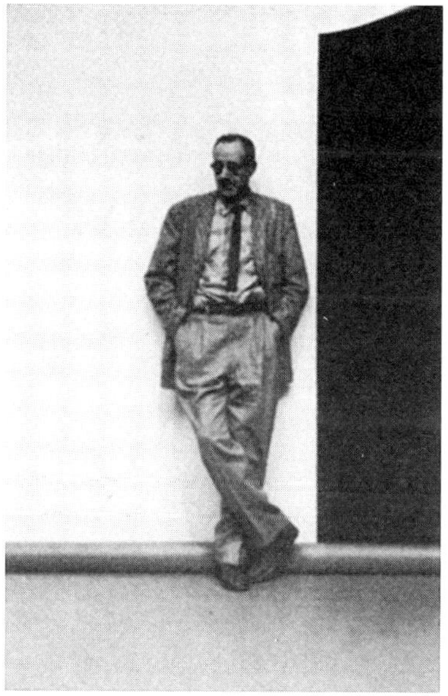

Photograph by Bruce Elkus.

EXERCISE

Mark off a series of equal-sized picture borders on several sheets of white paper. Cut a number of squares, circles and triangles out of any black paper. Try placing these in different positions and different relationships in each of the picture borders. When the arrangement, or the composition, feels right, paste them into place with rubber cement. Study the results and see if you can "feel" how each picture acts differently.

This should serve to stimulate and exercise your sensitivity to spatial relationships and their activity.

FLAT OR SHALLOW SPACE

Since the first picture was made, artists have been challenged with the problem of creating the illusion of space on a flat, two-dimensional surface. This has made available to us a rich reservoir of various technical means of achieving space.

All pictures can be divided roughly into two categories— flat space and deep space. Though many pictures combine these, generally one concept of space or the other is dominant. Most of pictorial art is primarily flat in spatial concept. Only for a limited time in relation to our total art history were pictures made with deep spatial emphasis. This was during the Renaissance, and from that period the theories of perspective evolved. This section of the book concentrates on two-dimentional composition, which dominates contemporary art thinking.

A sense of depth of space can be realized by using planes parallel to the picture frame (without perspective). It is apparent in the illustrated student exercises that they vary in feeling of depth and space. As the horizon, or eye level line, is raised, the sense of depth is increased. The partial overlapping of one subject on another tends to intensify the depth feeling.

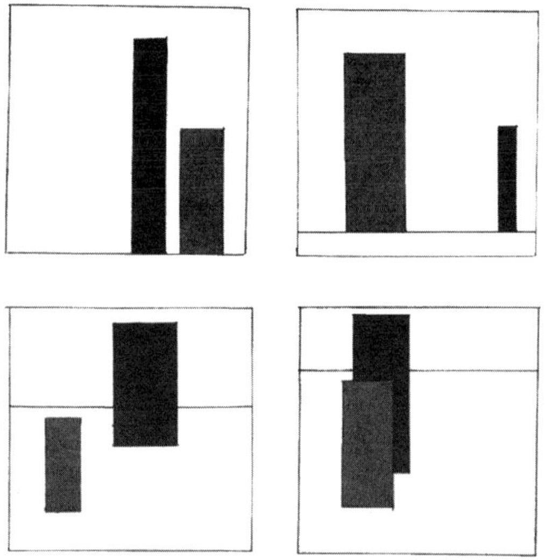

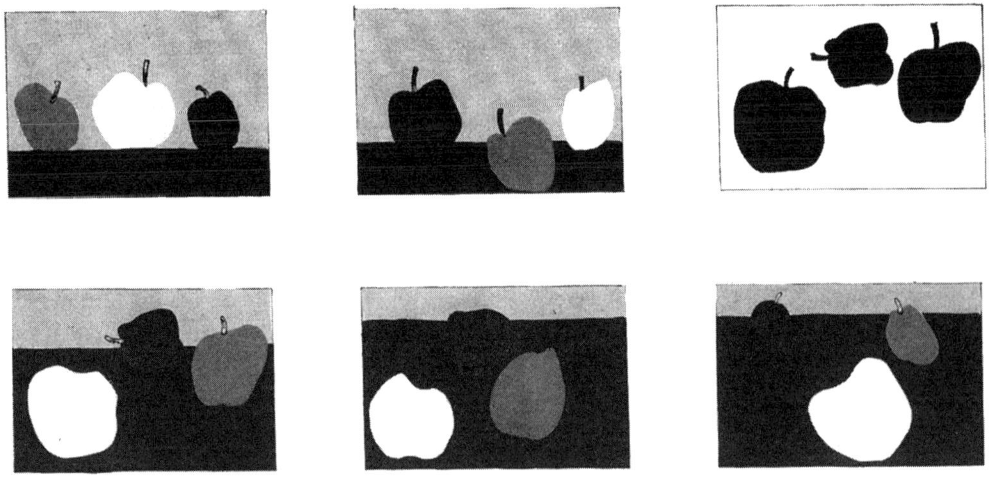

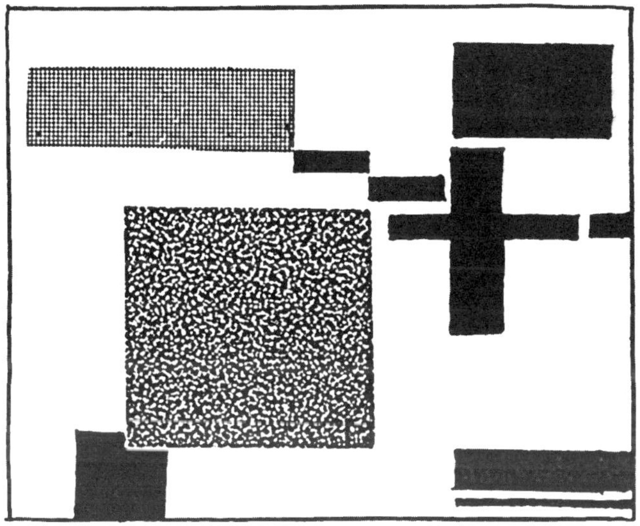

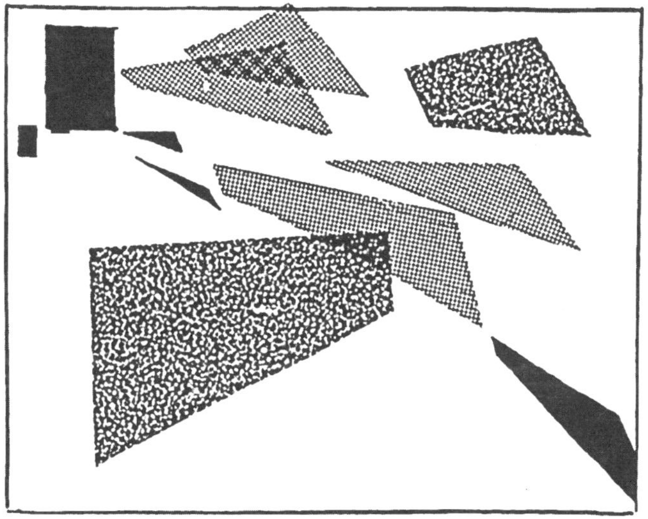

In one design exercise all the planes are vertical and horizontal to the borders of the picture. In the other a greater penetration of space results from tilting the planes into perspective depth. A deeper sense of space and greater spatial activity result.

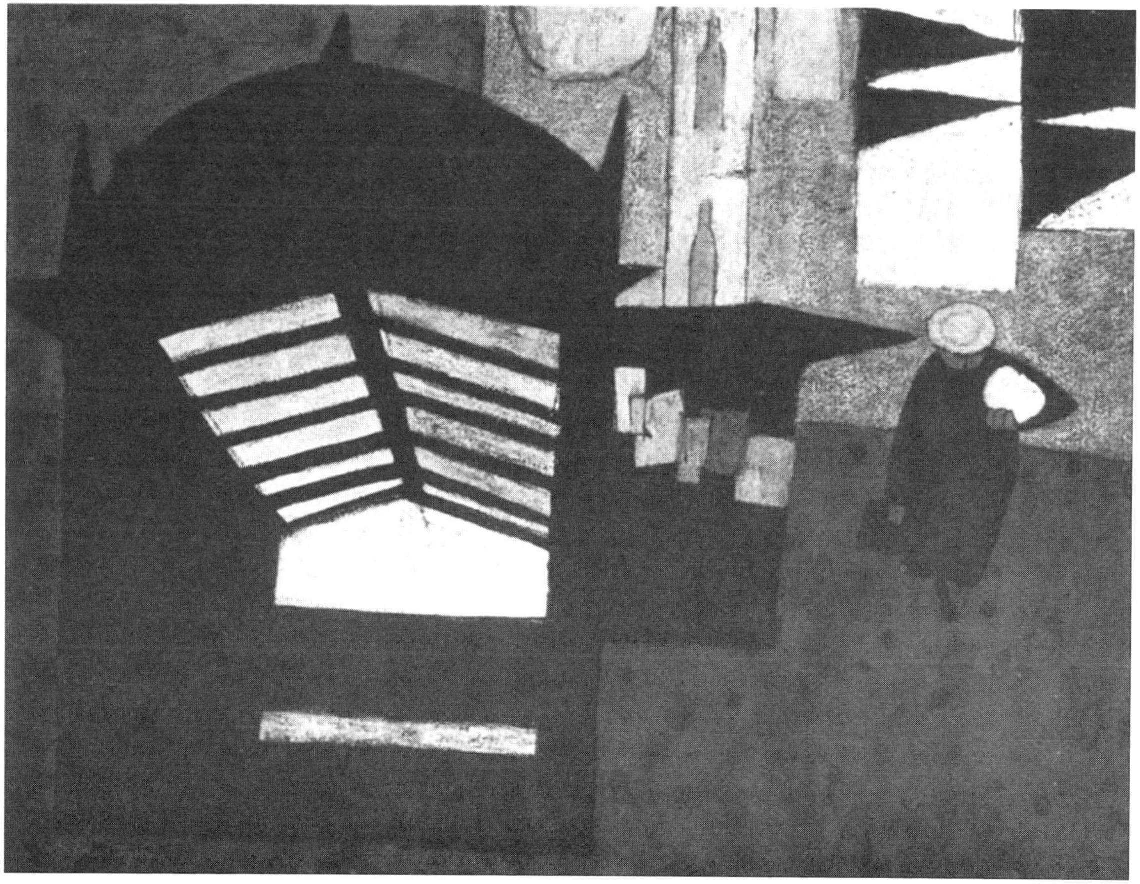

G. PRESTOPINO.
Subway.
ACA Gallery.

FLAT OR SHALLOW SPACE

The woodcut by Frasconi and the painting by Miro both use flat design with a shallow depth of spatial feeling. Both use overlapping planes for recessive space.

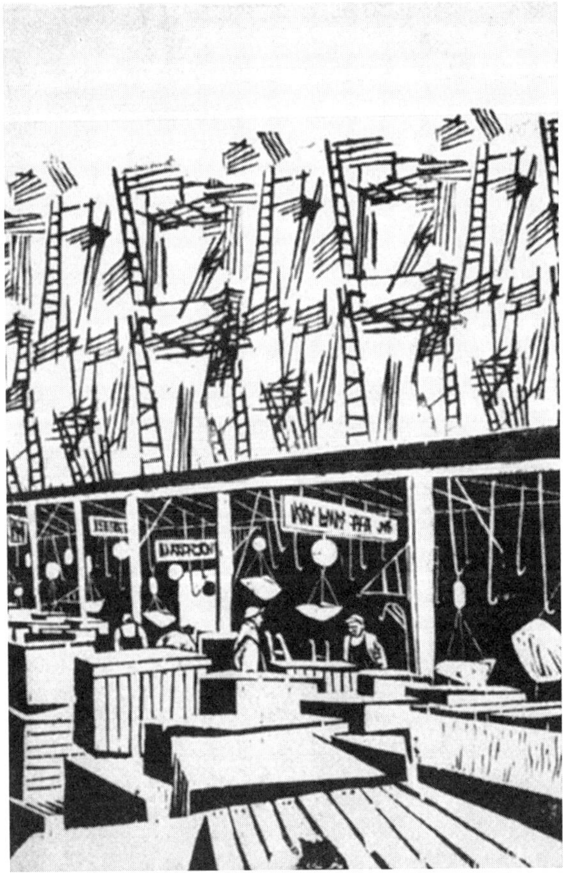

A. FRASCONI.
Detail from Fulton Fish Market (Cargo).
Weyhe Gallery.

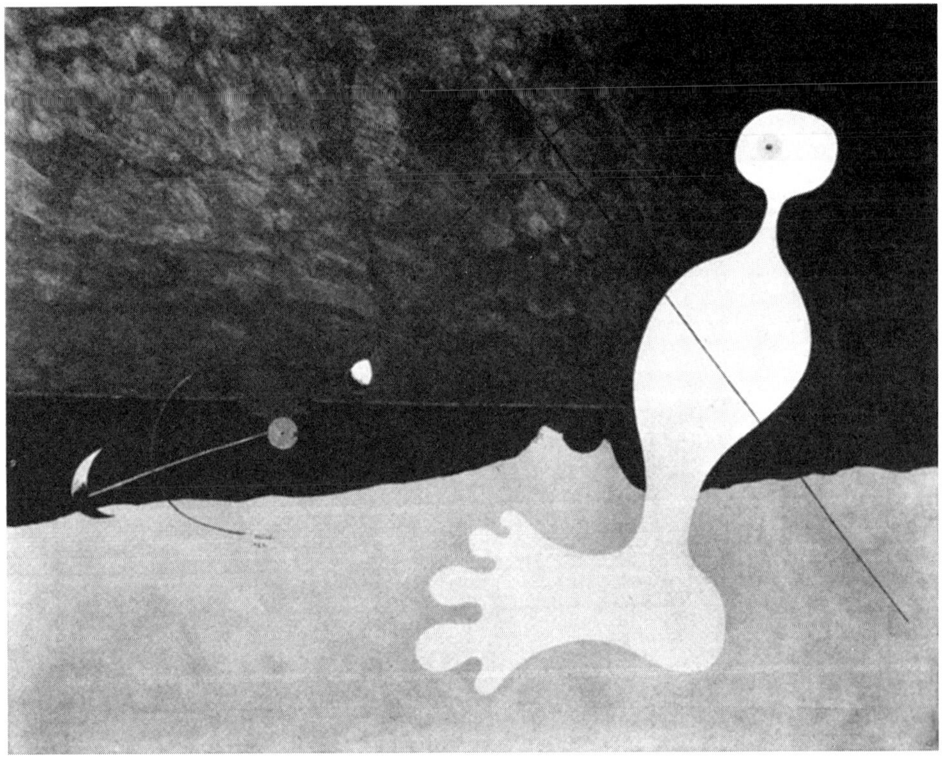

JOAN MIRO.
Person Throwing a Stone at a Bird.
Collection Museum of Modern Art.

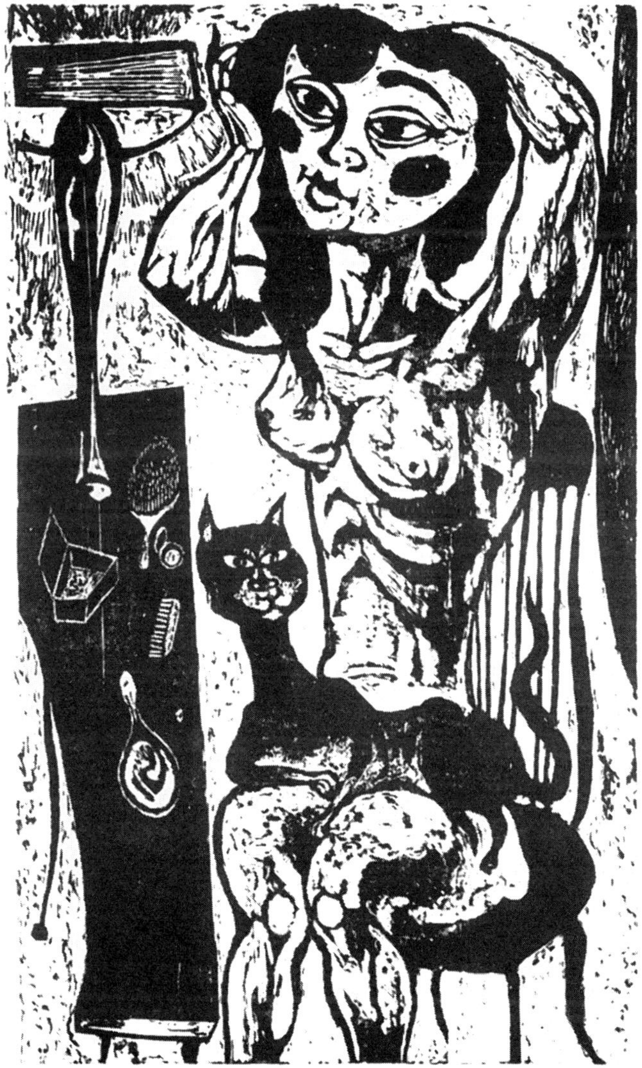

H. STERNBERG.
The Dressing Table.
ACA Gallery.

FLAT OR SHALLOW SPACE

It is interesting to note the influence of Western design on the Eastern picture reproduced below.

The flattening of the perspective in the dressing table in the Sternberg woodcut serves to retain the shallow space of the rest of the picture.

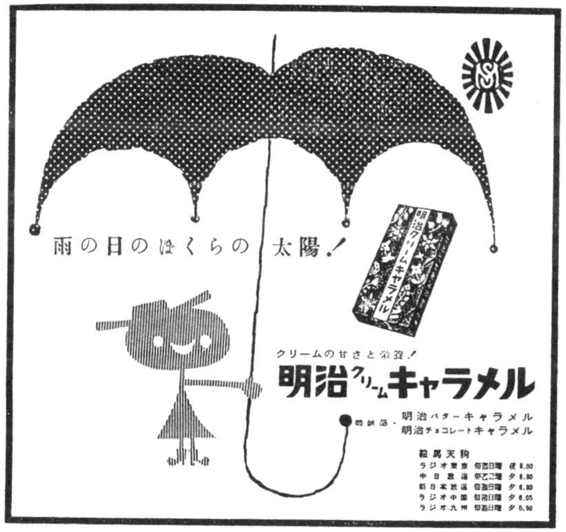

EXERCISE

Arrange a still life with a few simple objects. On several sheets of paper draw picture borders—some vertical and some horizontal. Inside one of these do a line drawing of the still life as you see it. On the other pages do several versions of the still life without moving the objects. Shift their relationship to each other and to the border. Raise and lower the table line. Study the compositions for spatial feeling. Do design exercises as illustrated on the previous page.

POSITIVE AND NEGATIVE SPACE

The borders of a picture, the picture frame, enclose a defined area of space, generally considered as negative space. The shapes or objects placed in the picture create positive space, and the remaining area is negative space. The interrelationship between these two is one of the dynamics of composition. Sole concentration on the positive elements, the figure, vase or tree, inevitably results in compositional inadequacy. The artist must be conscious of both types of space when he designs his picture.

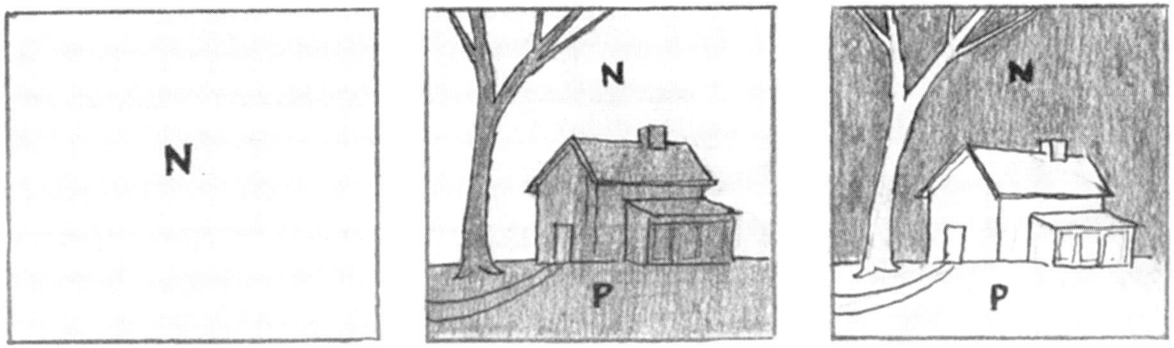

The two examples on the right demonstrate how negative space can be analyzed. The negative spaces in both are intensely active and visually sensuous.

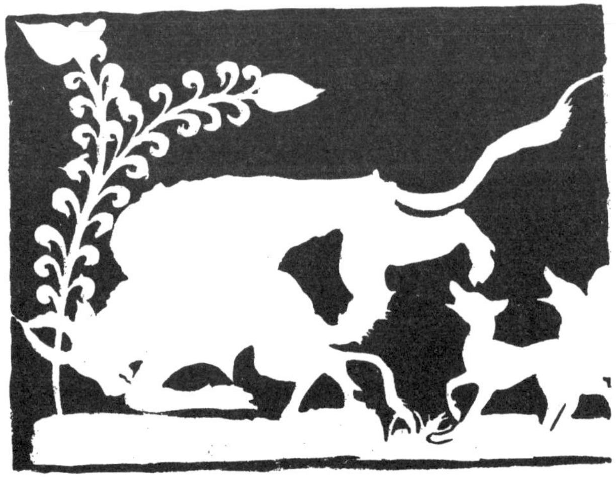

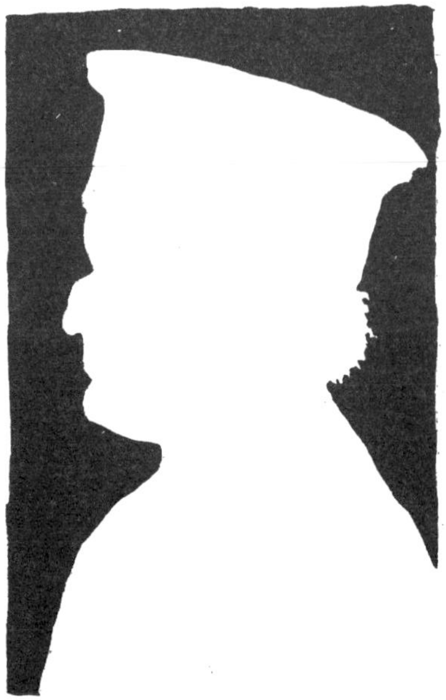

The picture is analyzed for positive and negative space to illustrate this design principle. In one the total positive area is depicted with black. In the other the negative area is blacked in.

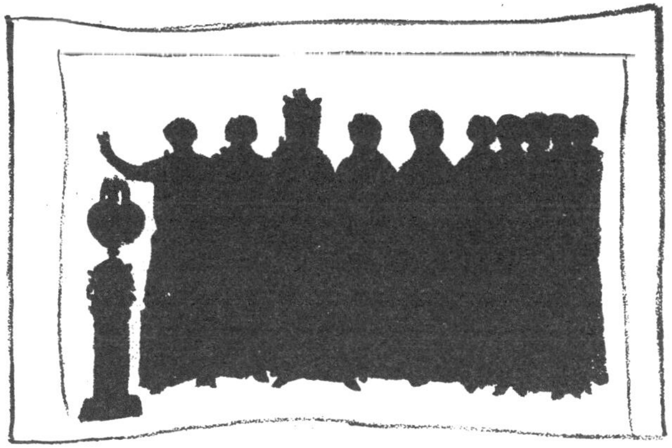

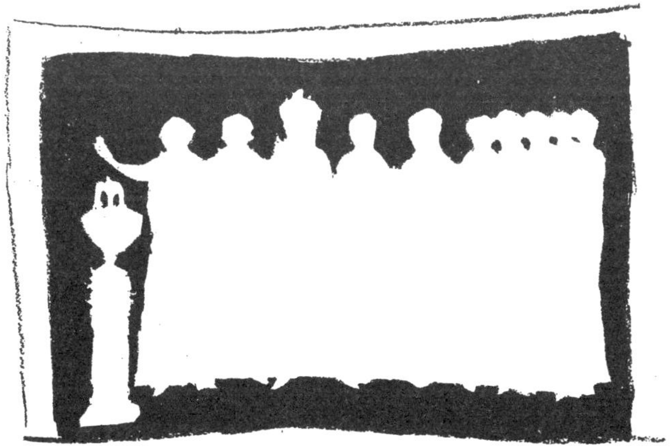

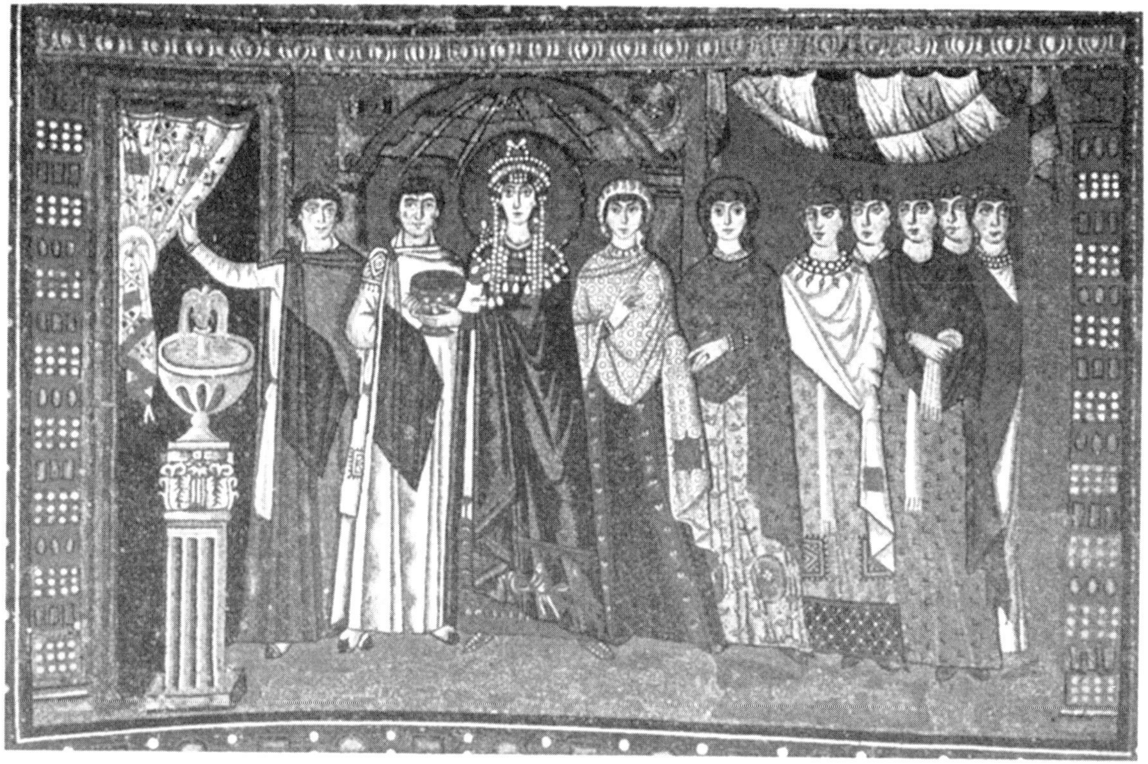

Detail from a Byzantine Mosaic.

POSITIVE AND NEGATIVE SPACE

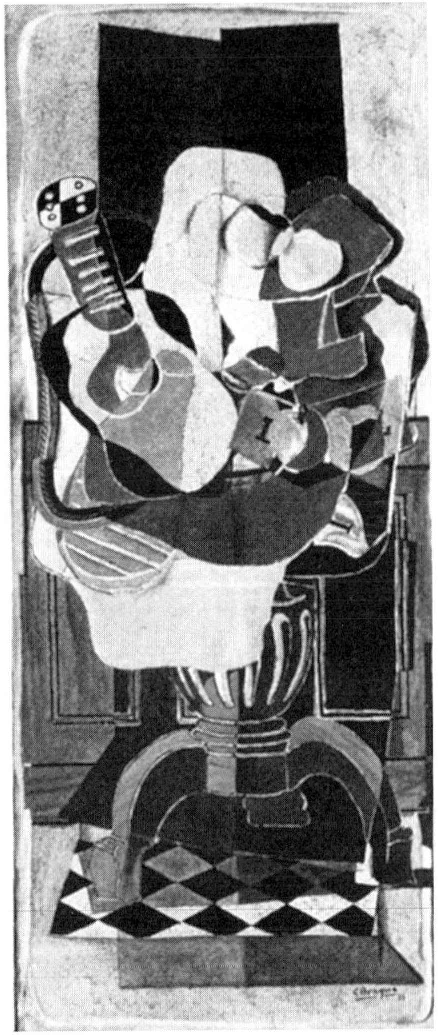

G. BRAQUE.
The Table.
Collection Museum of Modern Art.

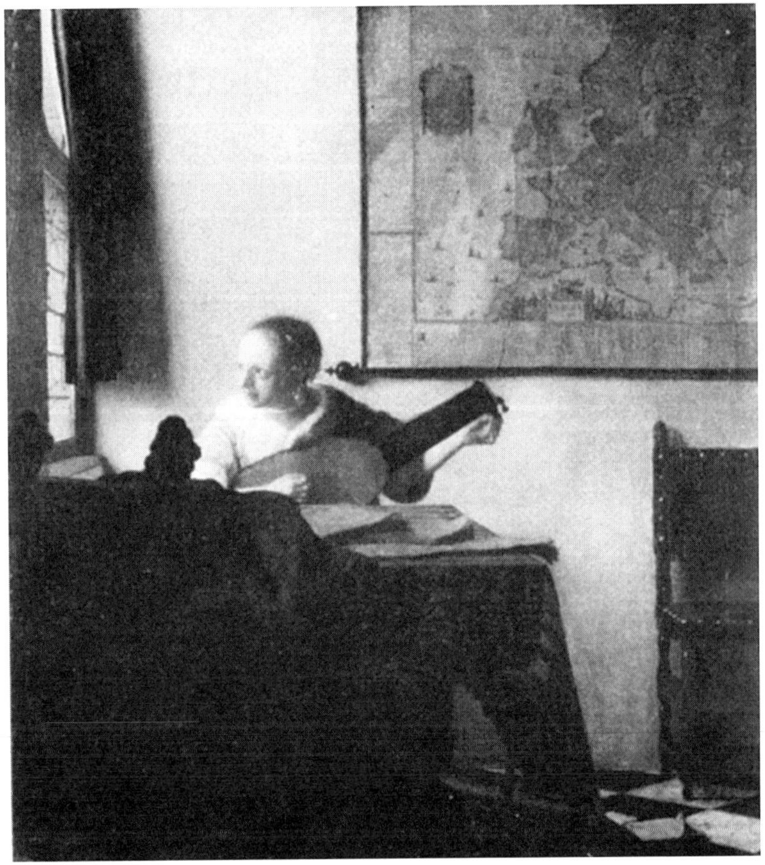

VERMEER.
Lady with a Lute.
Metropolitan Museum of Art.

EXERCISE

Choose some reproductions of painting by old or contemporary masters. Use tracing paper or acetate. First, trace and mass in with black the positive areas. Then do the same with the negative areas. Study the results. Try this on your own pictures.

Tension is a term used to describe the attraction and repulsion of elements in a composition. This spatial sensation of activity can be used not only to create a dynamically alive picture, but also to intensify the communicativeness of a picture.

The student exercises illustrate optical communication of verticalness, ascent and descent, depth of space, and compression and expansion.

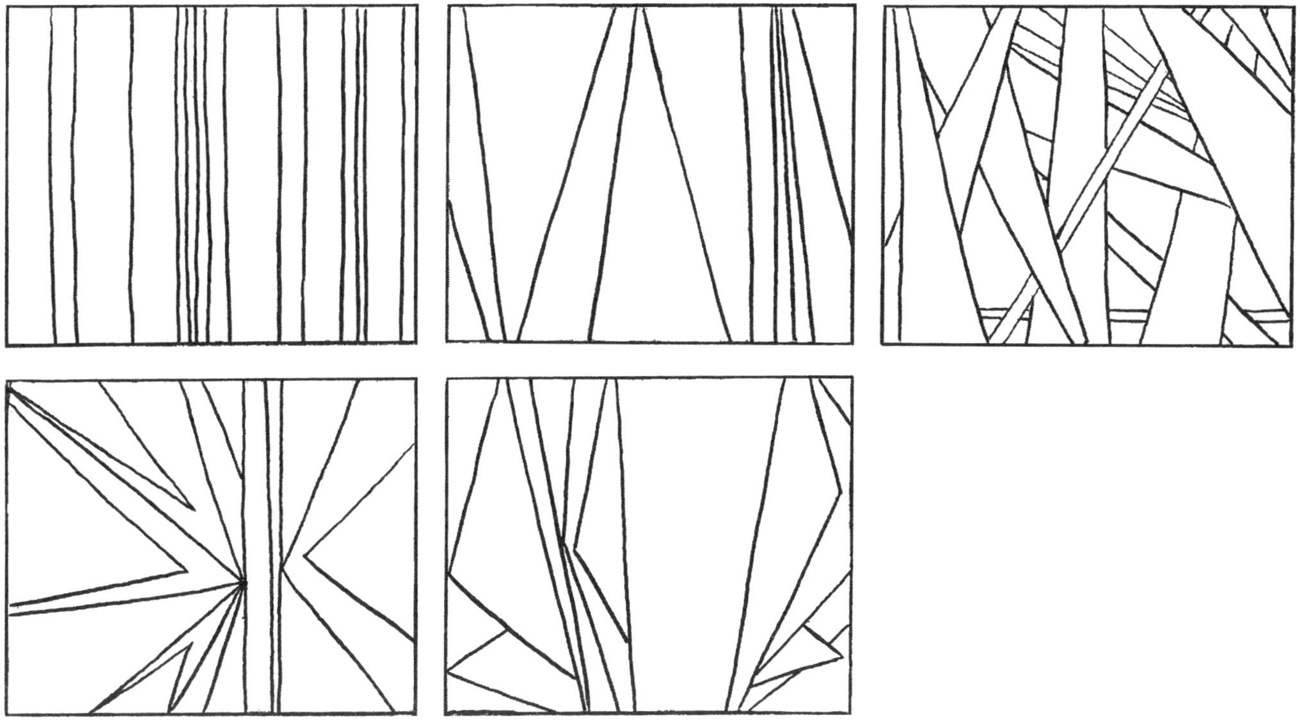

THE ACTIVITY OF SHAPES

The action of balance and imbalance, the sense of movement about to happen, as shown in the designs below, involve the use of the square, circle and triangle. These three basic forms are capable as well of visual statements of action and tension by themselves. By changing their shapes and directional thrusts, the nature of the squareness or roundness is kept, but each is capable of a variety of spatial expressions.

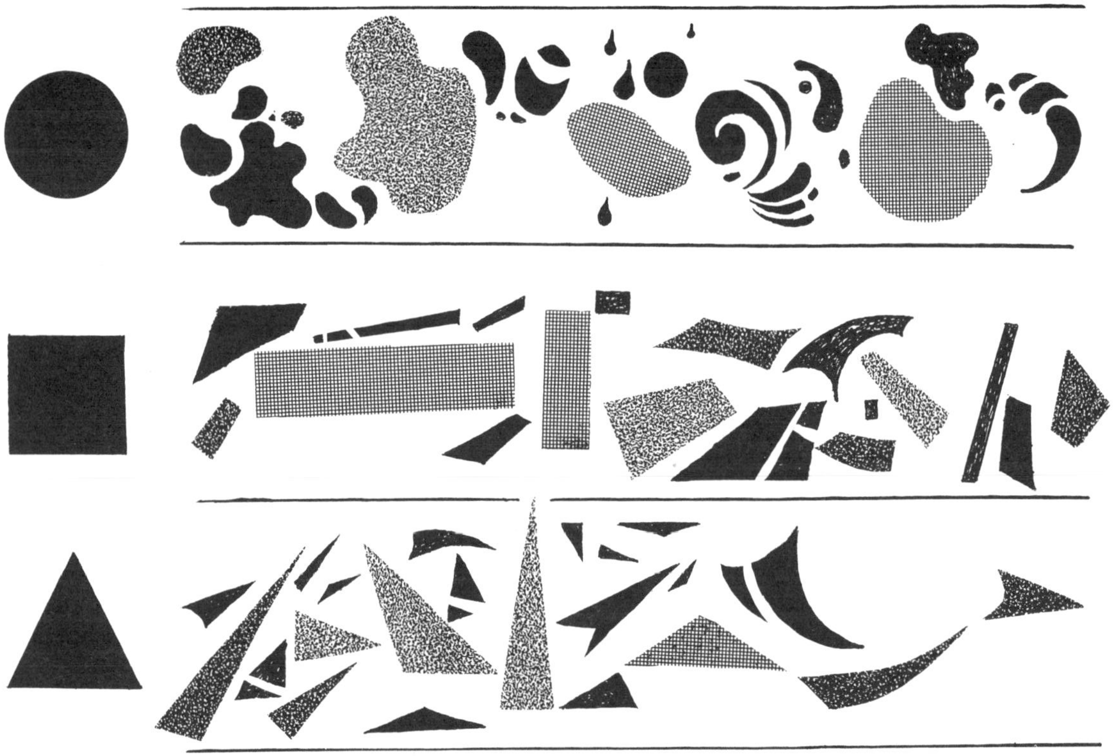

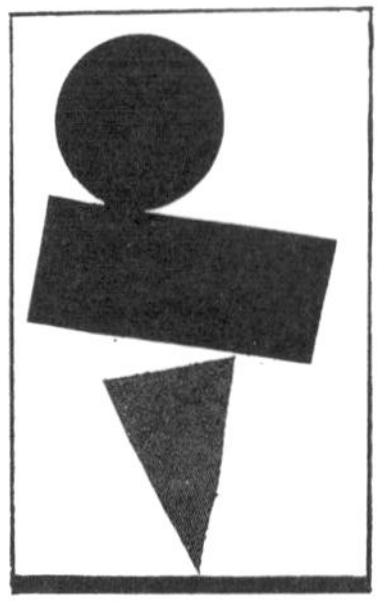

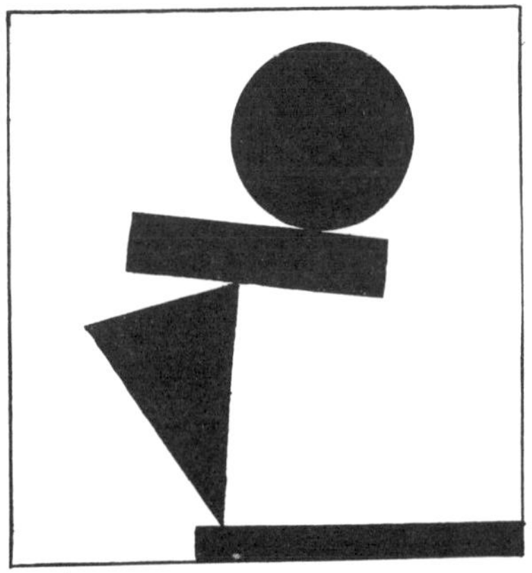

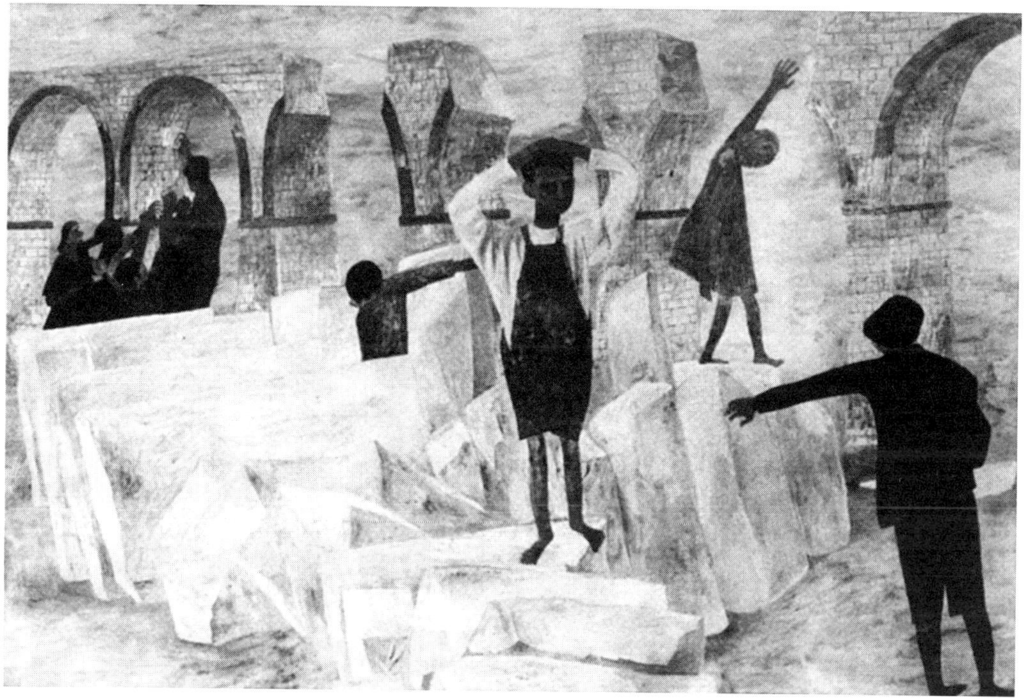

BEN SHAHN.
Reconstruction.
Whitney Museum of Art.

JACOB LAWRENCE.
The River.
Alan Gallery.

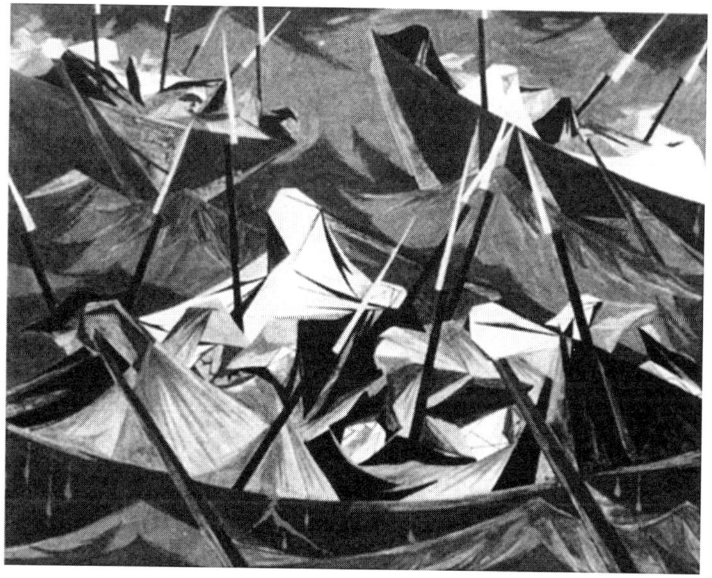

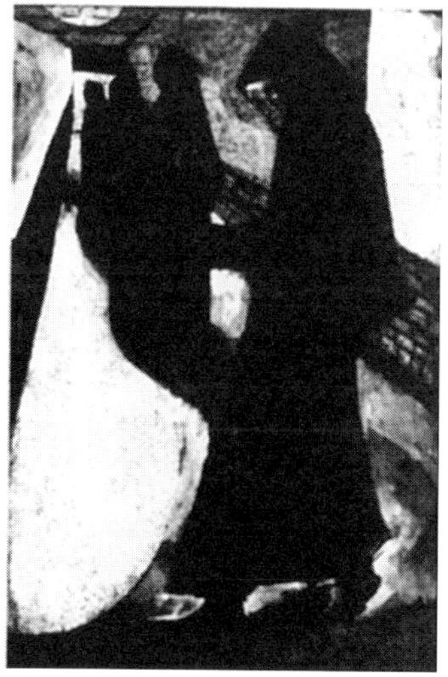

J. BILANDER.
The Procession.
Courtesy of the Artist.

THE ACTIVITY OF SHAPES

The three exercises on this page demonstrate the ability of design to express smallness and largeness, movement and space, and crowded jostling.

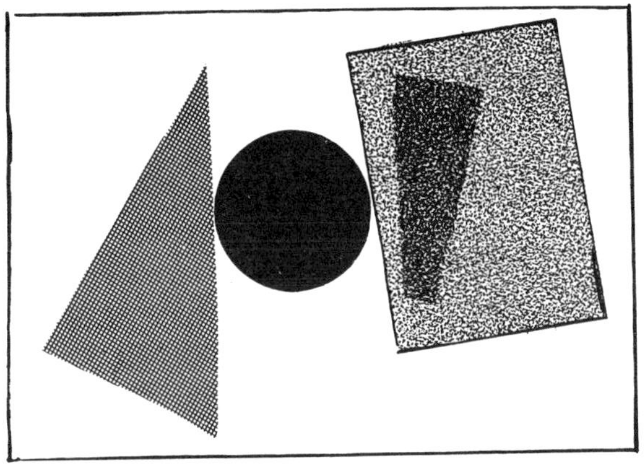

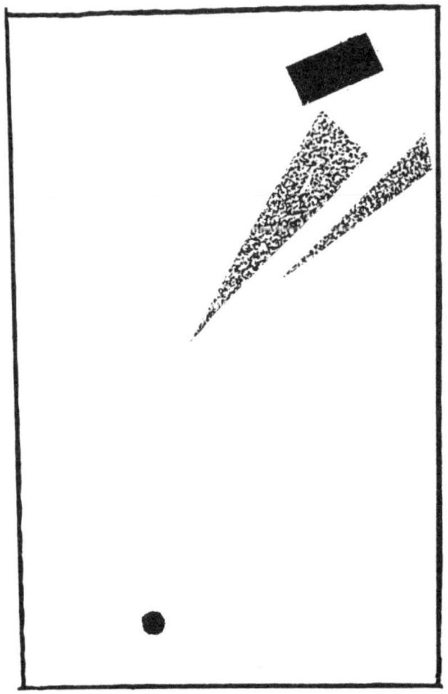

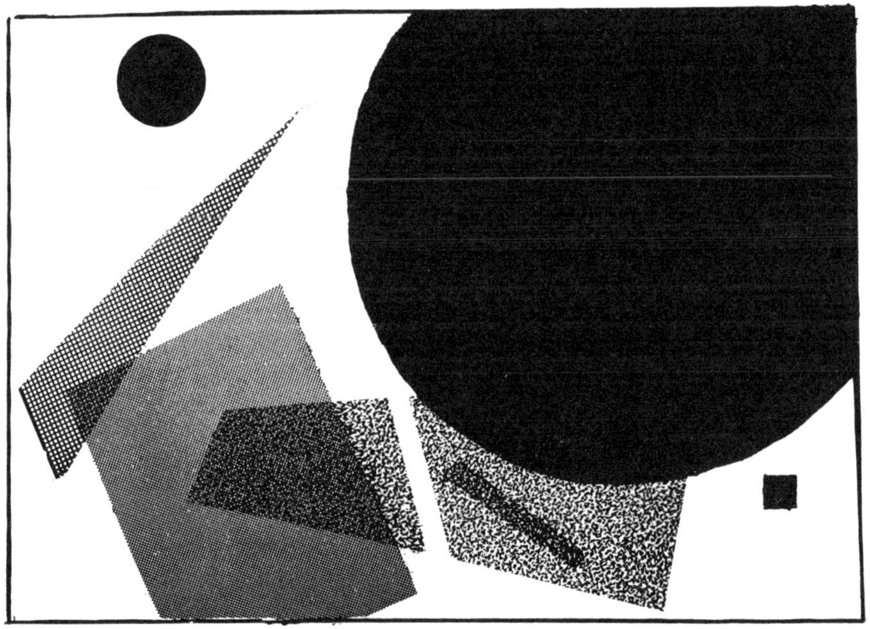

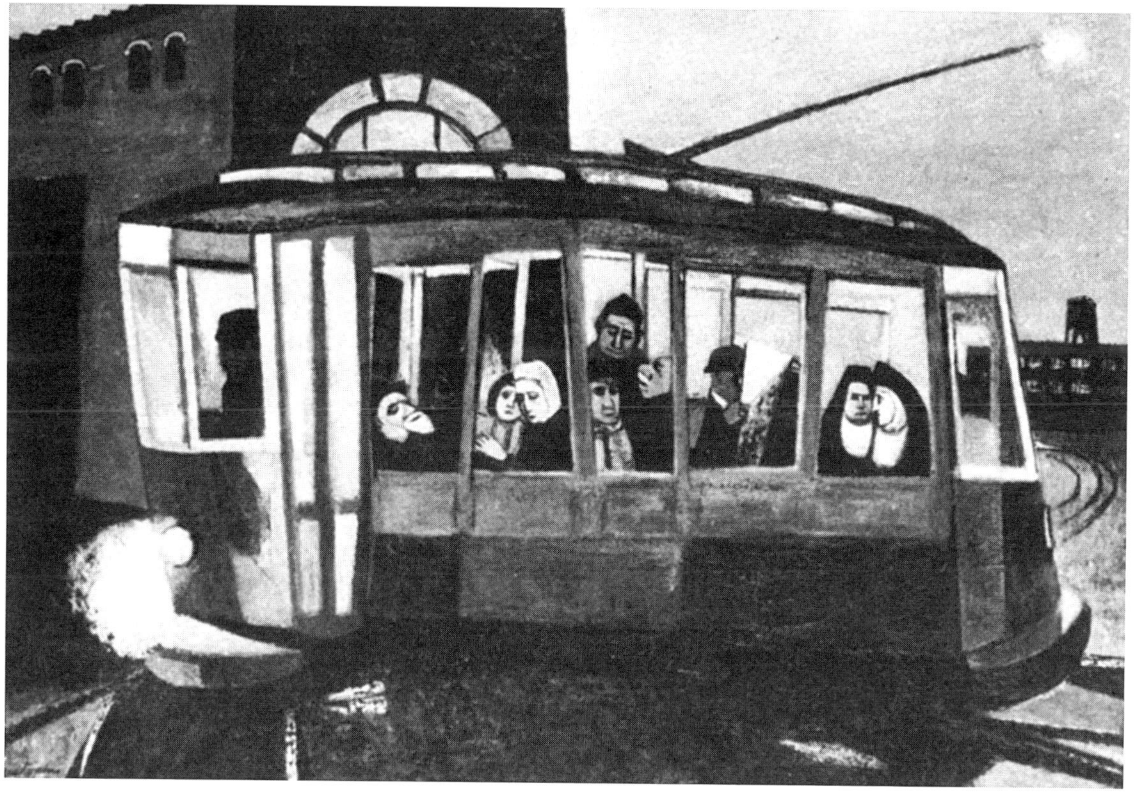

G. PRESTOPINO.
Trolley.
ACA Gallery.

J. ERNST.
Lookscape.
Grace Borgenicht Gallery.

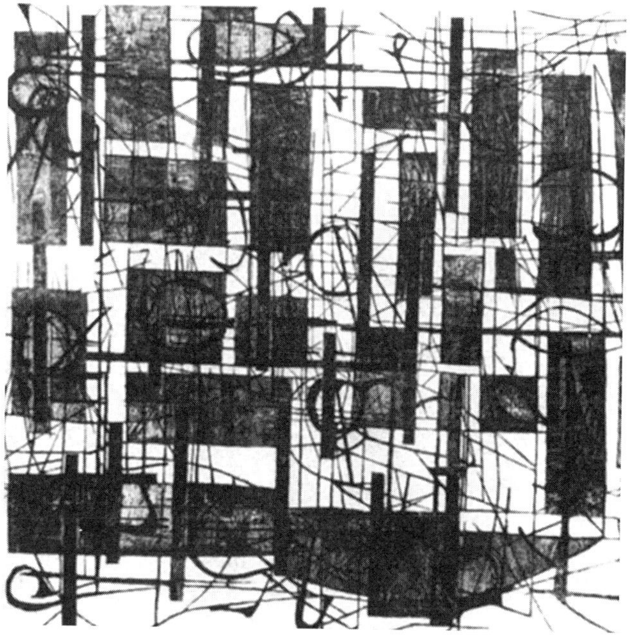

THE ACTIVITY OF SHAPES

By using black and white values, it is obvious that a white object in the foreground can be projected by making the background dark, or vice versa. The movement of the blacks and whites is limited by the outlines of the forms.

By interweaving the blacks and whites so that they move from one element of the design into another, a sense of relatedness is felt and a rich visual movement of tone is made possible.

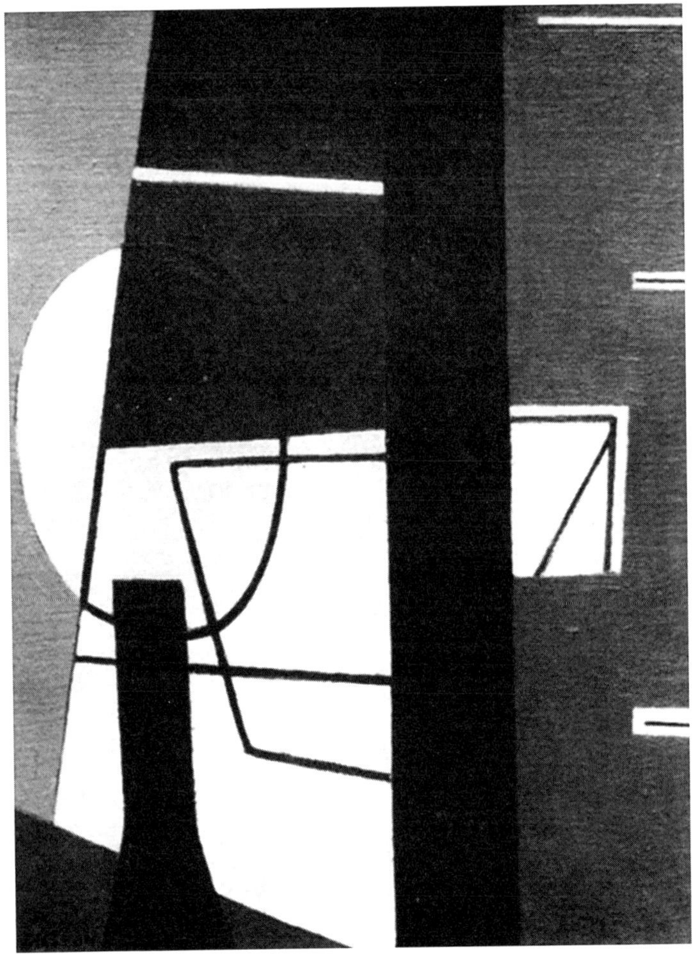

R. CRAWFORD.
Fishing Boat No. I.
Grace Borgenicht Gallery.

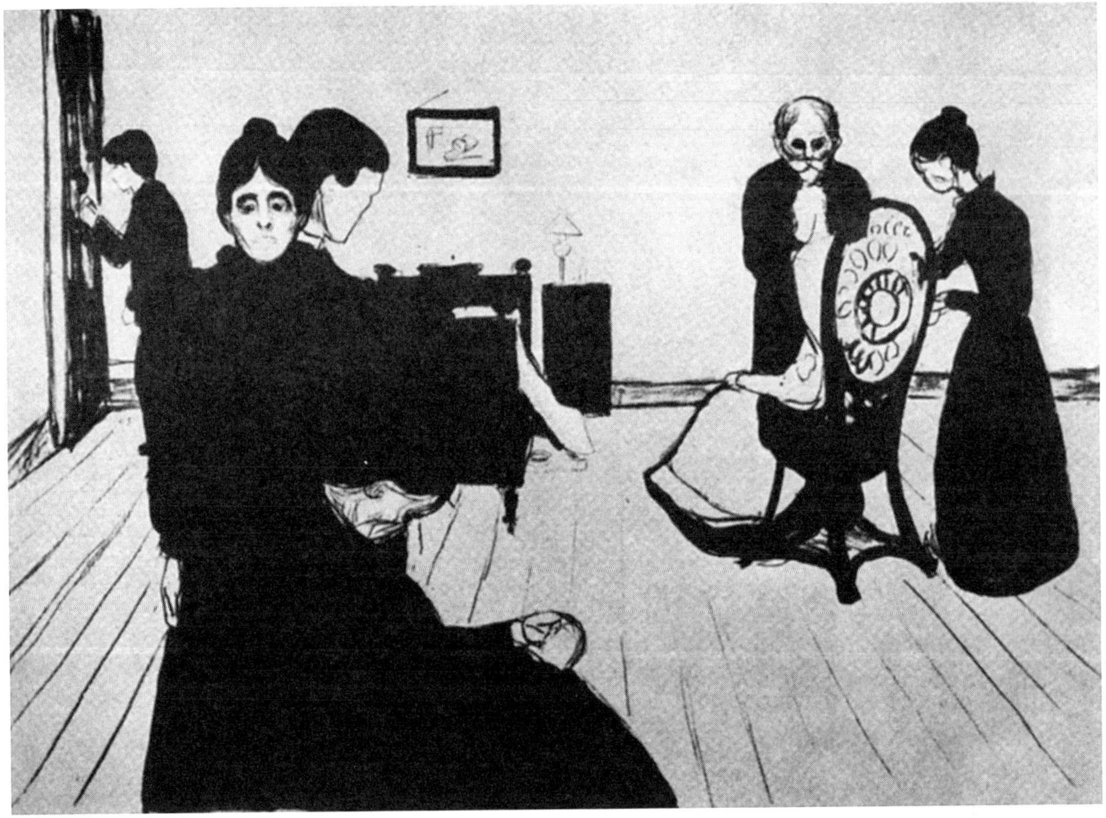

E. MUNCH.
Death Chamber.

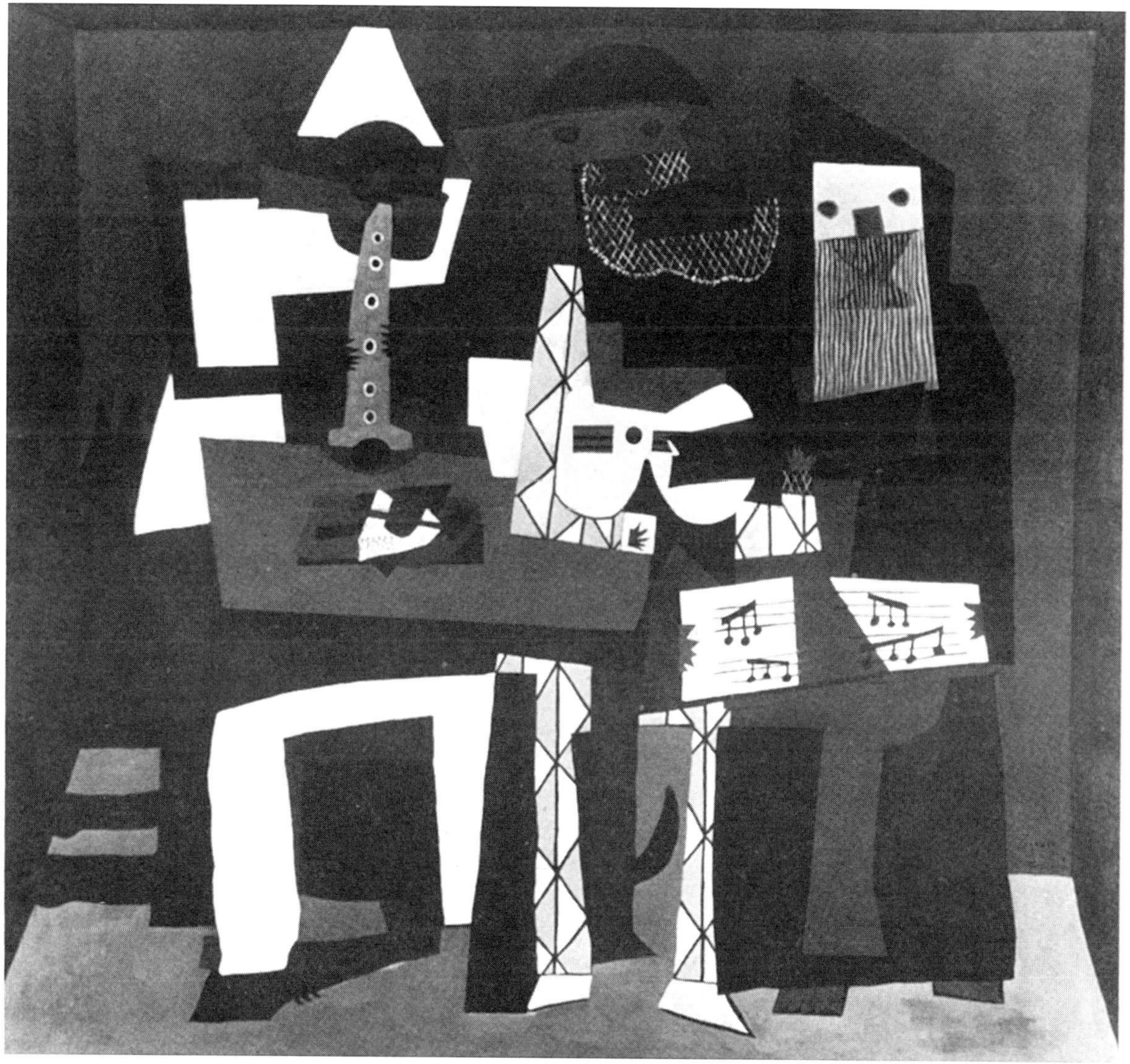

PICASSO.
Three Musicians.
Collection Museum of Modern Art.

This painting incorporates many of the design principles discussed in the previous chapters.

THE ACTIVITY OF SHAPES

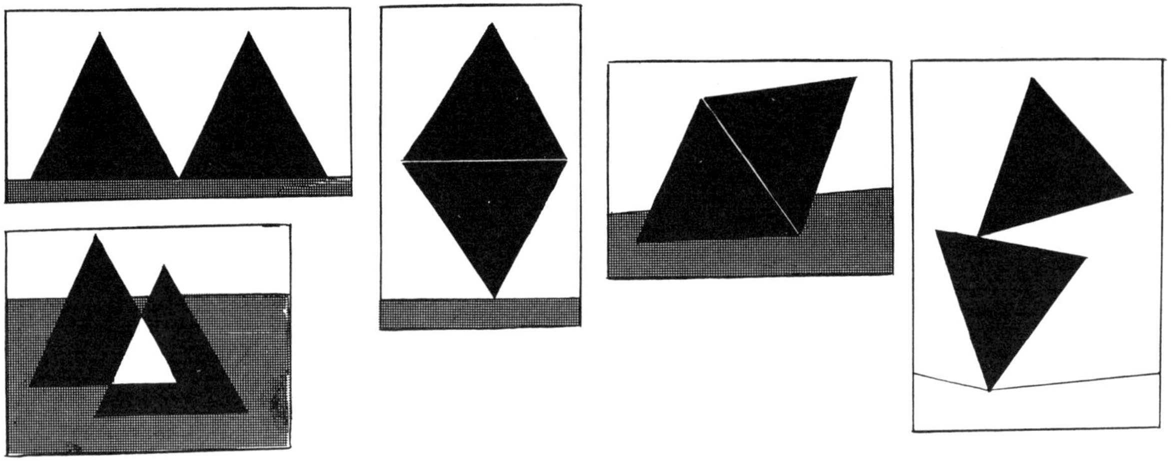

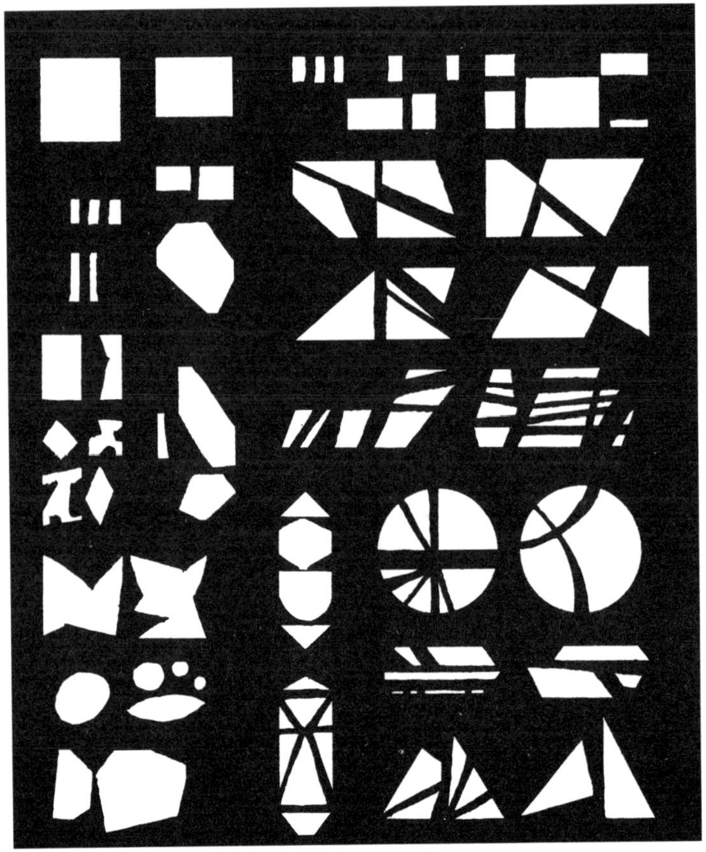

The design exercise above demonstrates how the relationship of objects changes the very meaning of the objects. The two triangles used in different relationships assume not only new activity, but new significance as well.

To the left is an exercise in which the student is searching for variations on the basic square, circle and triangle.

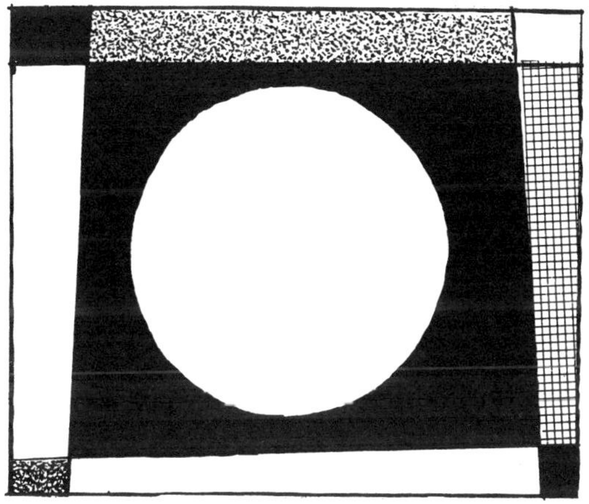

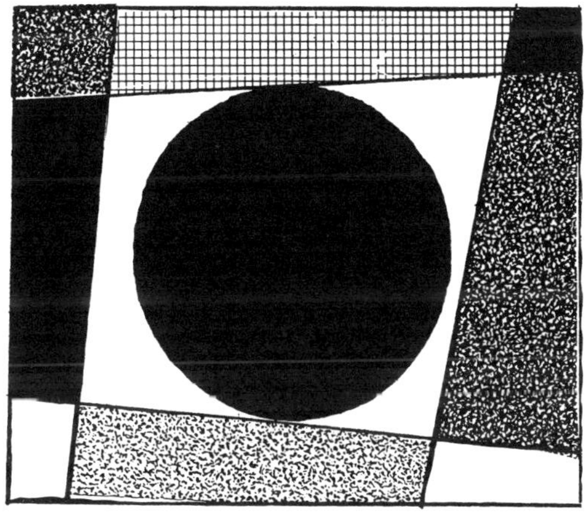

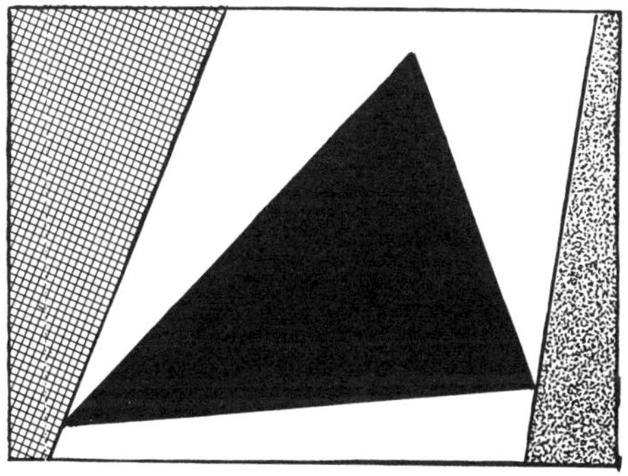

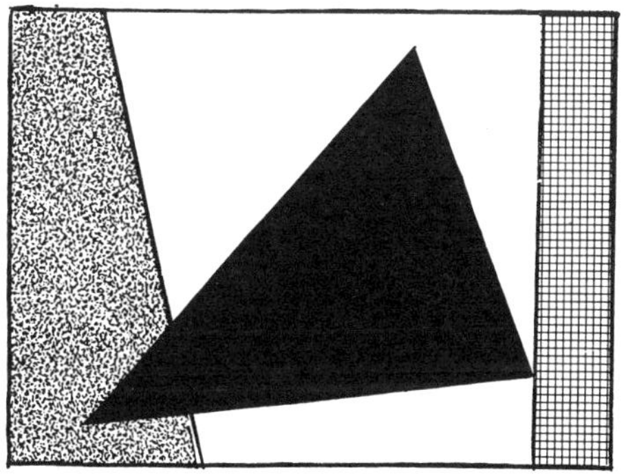

EXERCISE

This chapter has dealt with many aspects of the activity of shapes in space. Each of the student exercises shown is a study of one aspect of design. Work out your own studies of tension, using lines only. Experiment with various combinations of squares, circles and triangles for scale, movement and balance. Study and analyze pictures for interweaving blacks and whites. Do each of the exercises in many different ways until you understand and can control the principles.

VALUES

Values are the range of tones beginning with white and running through the scale of grays and middle tones to black. Values afford the artist additional implements to serve his compositional needs.

That a tonal value has no meaning except when related to a background is demonstrated in the exercise below. The square of middletone changes with each change of tonal environment.

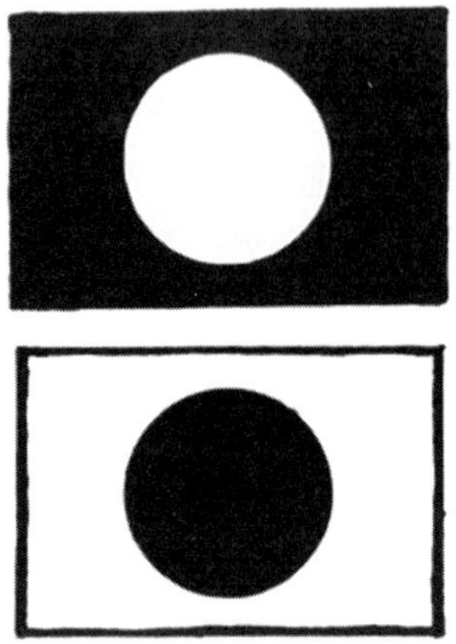

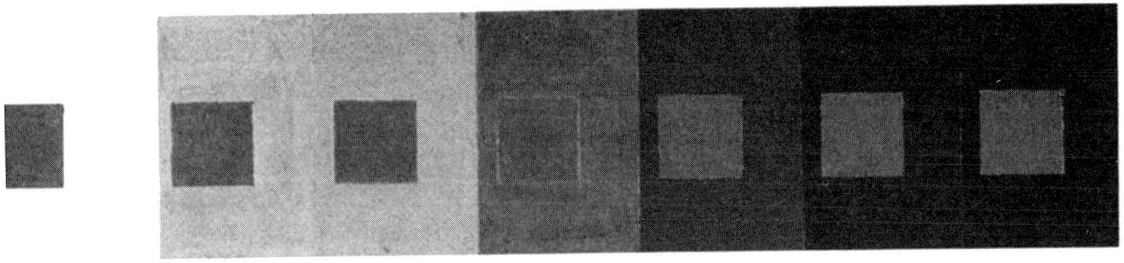

The observer's eye can be guided and directed to any part of a picture at the artist's will by use of tonal contrasts.

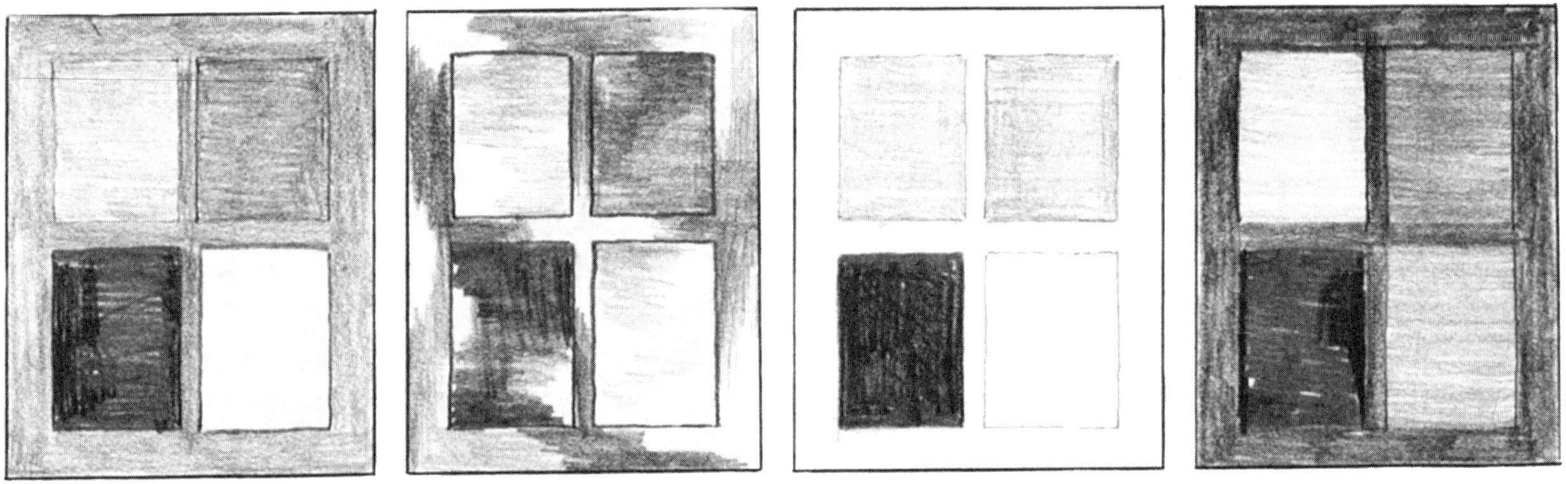

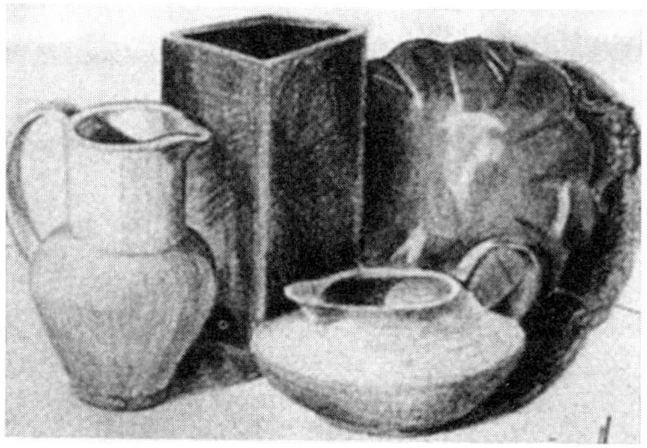

The still life studies to the left are a class problem in values. The top study is a copy of the objects done academically and naturalistically. In the second study arbitrary black and white decisions have been made for design and balance. The third study has been carried further from naturalism, using transparency as a design extension.

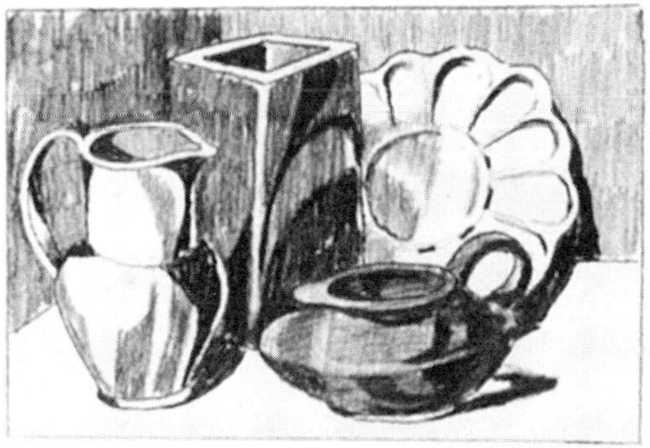

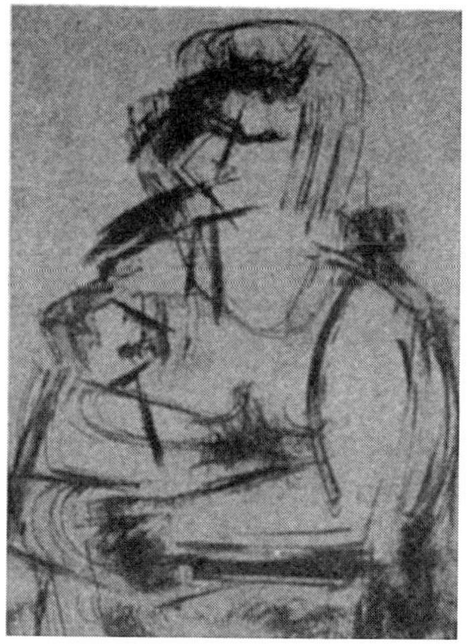

This group of pictures was made by N. Musi. Using a technique which he originated, he began with a drawing of a mother and child and developed the pictures with a photostat camera.

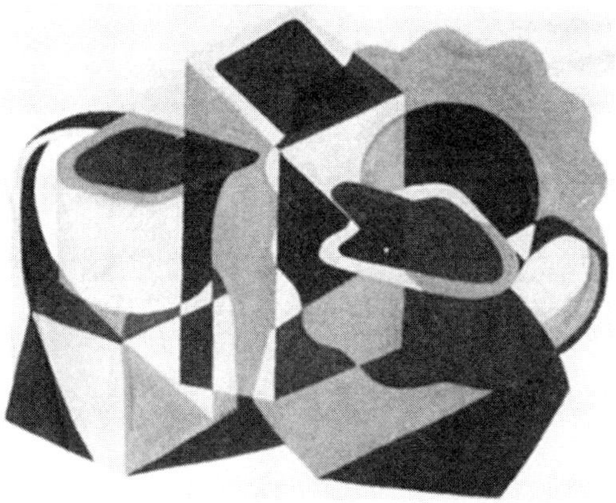

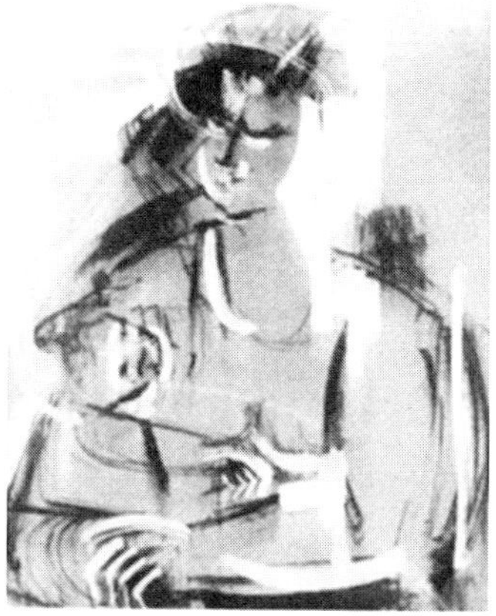

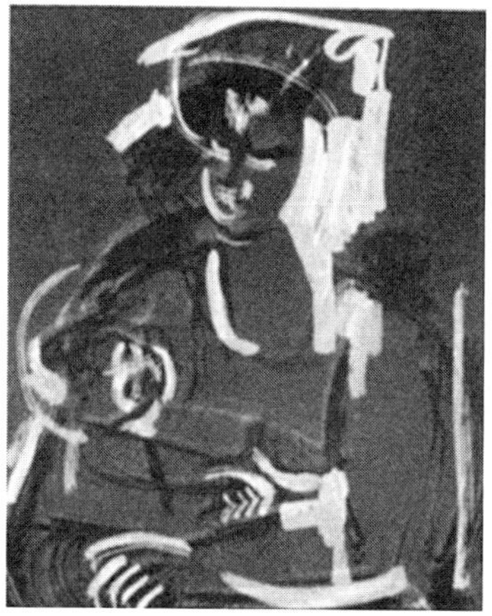

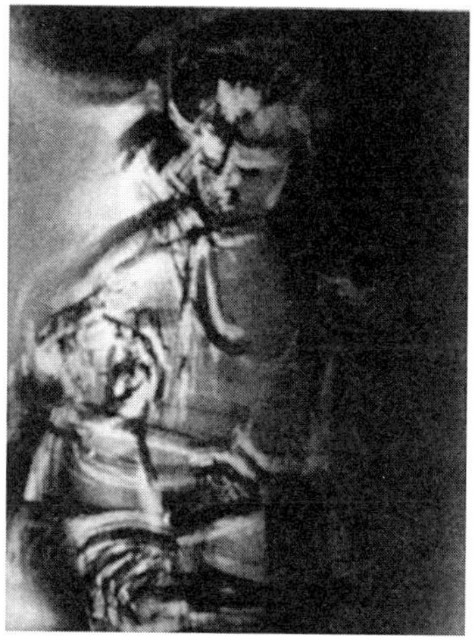

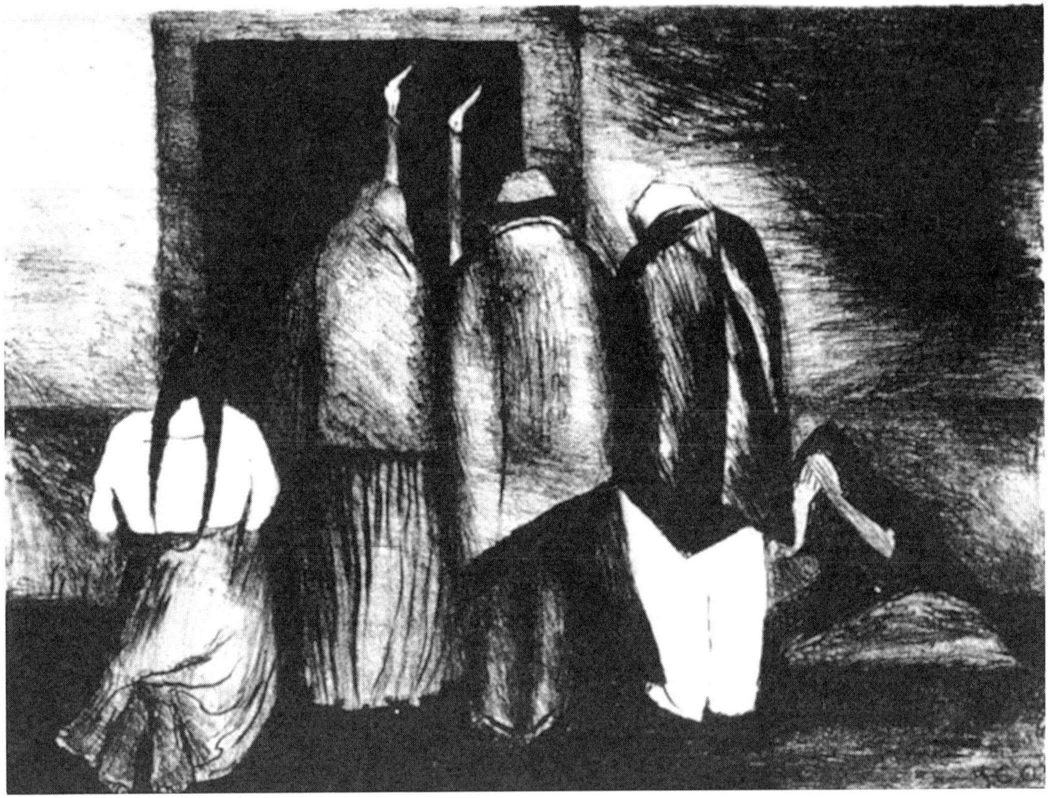

OROZCO.
Requiem.
Philadelphia Museum of Art.

The picture has been analyzed by eliminating details and reducing shapes and values to their basic structures.

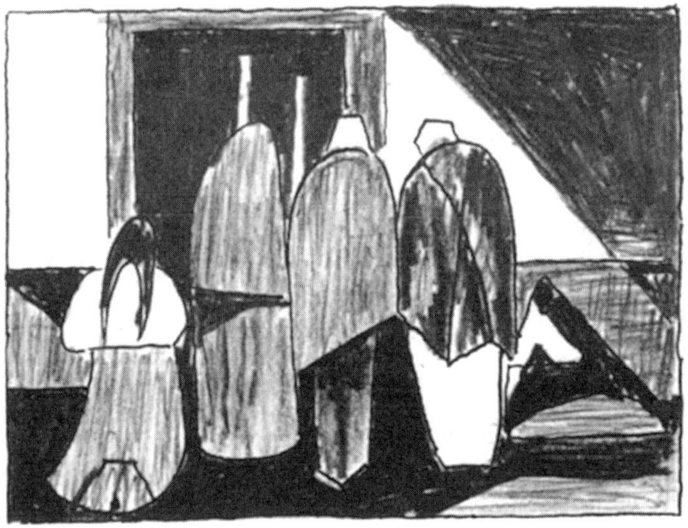

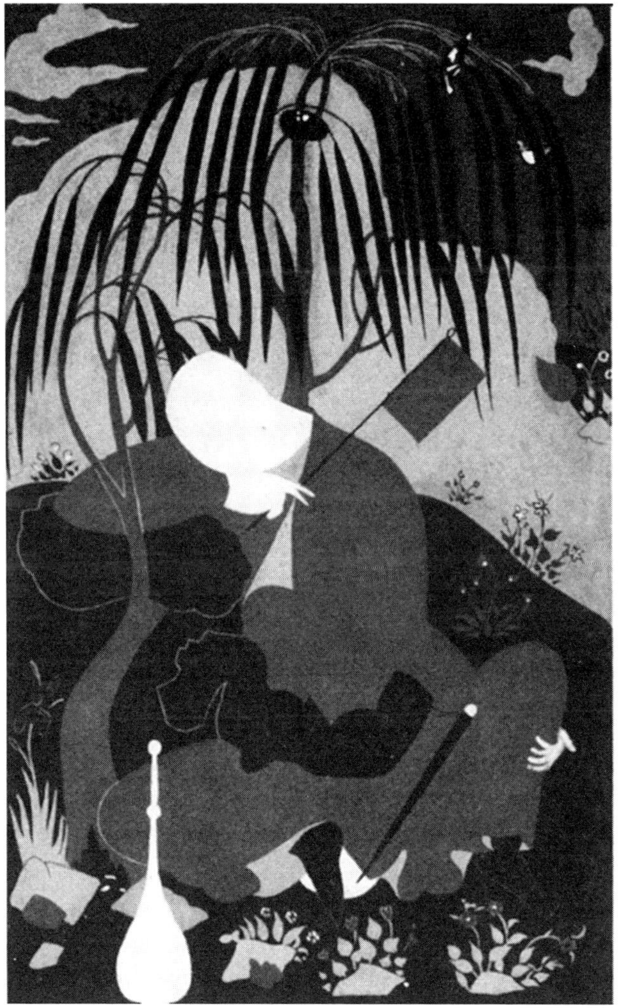

The 16th century Persian painting and the 20th century Orozco analyzed on this page show the similarity of concern with flat pattern for design.

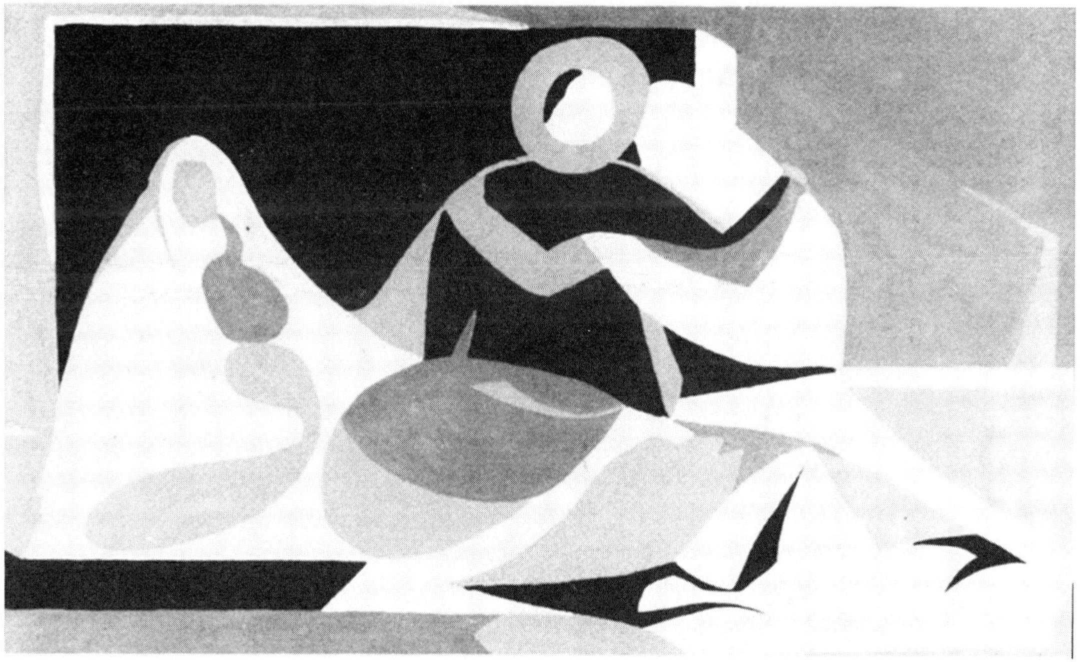

EXERCISE

Paint, with tempera, a series of squares ranging in tone from light gray to black. On each square paint an identical gray and then a middle value. Note how the value will change in each square.

Make a composition in values. Trace it three times. Change the values around in each picture. See which is most expressive.

The effective part that design plays in communication has been touched upon in previous chapters. It is necessary to enlarge on this because of the important role design plays in picture making.

The class problem illustrated was to begin with a picture and then reverse all the picture's values. In making this change the scene was transformed from a summer scene to a winter one. Then the original picture was cut apart and all the shapes were pasted down into an abstract design.

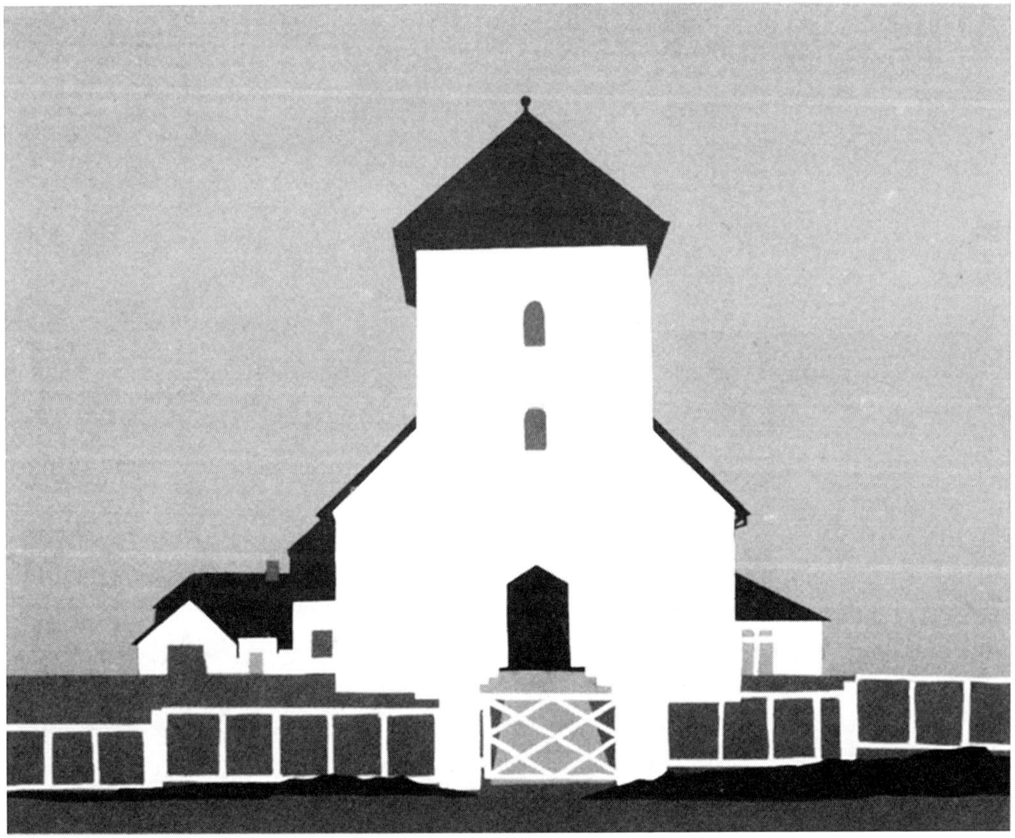

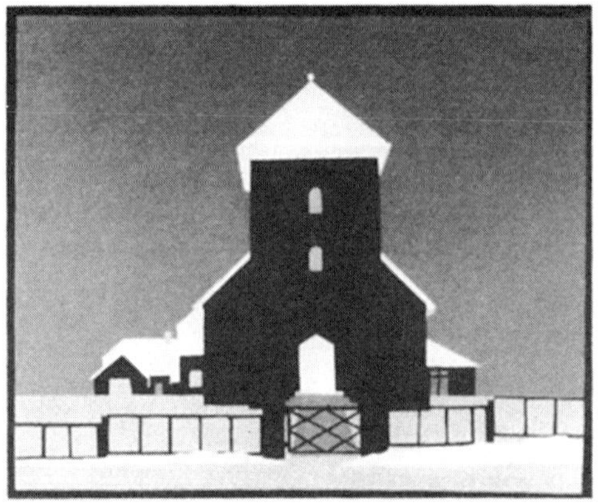

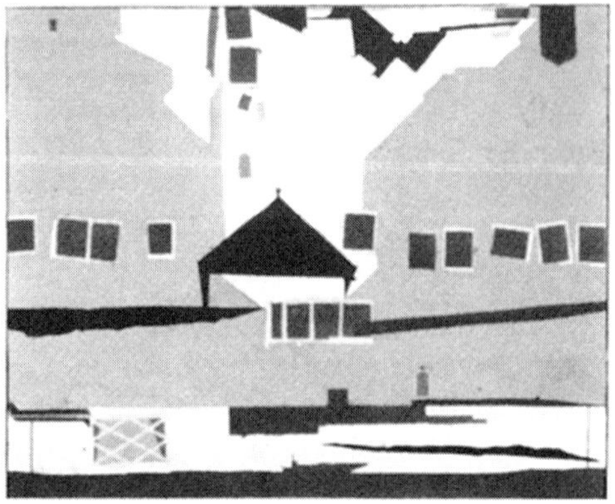

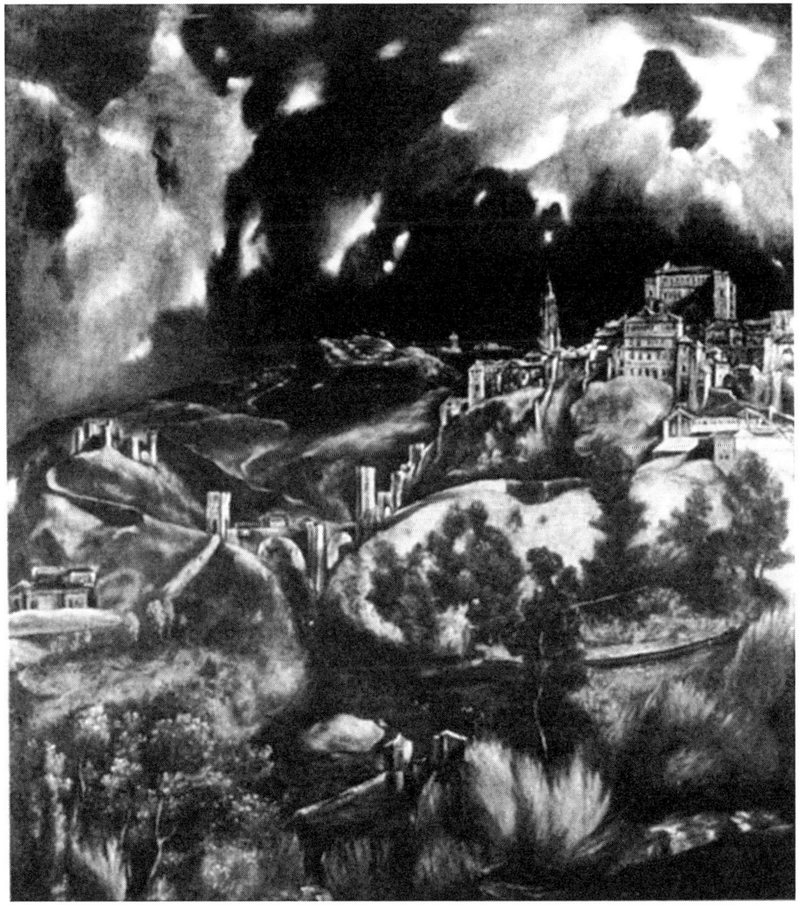

EL GRECO.
View of Toledo.
Metropolitan Museum of Art.

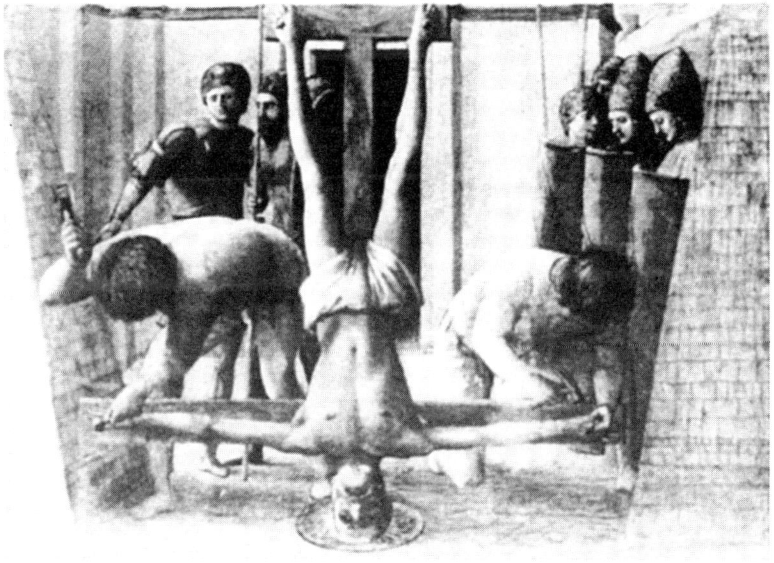

MASACCIO.
Detail from Martyrdom of St. Peter and John the Baptist.
Berlin Gallery.
Photo Courtesy of Metropolitan Museum of Art.

EXERCISE

Do the student problems explained and illustrated in this chapter.

To develop a more sensitive design feeling the exercise of making pictures in a few simple tonal values, cutting out the shapes and then pasting them down in abstract arrangements, is recommended.

The two pictures above are offered for analysis.

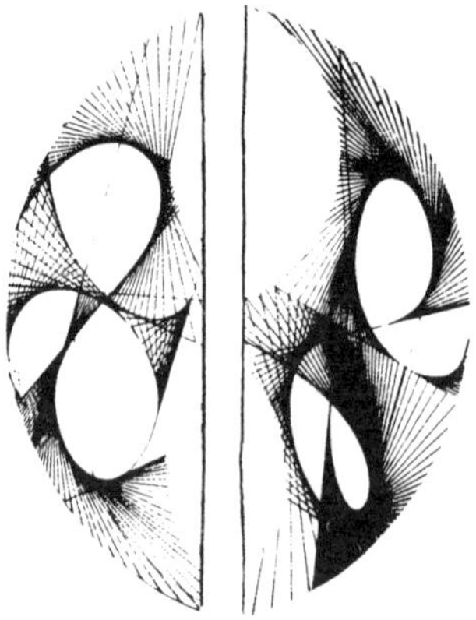

Although composition can be divided roughly into two major groups, flat space and deep space, there are many gradations between these extremes, and often both design concepts appear in one picture.

With the development of the principle of perspective during the Renaissance artists involved themselves with volume and deep space.

The modern movement has turned to primitive sources for inspiration, and with this has come a return to the use of flat space.

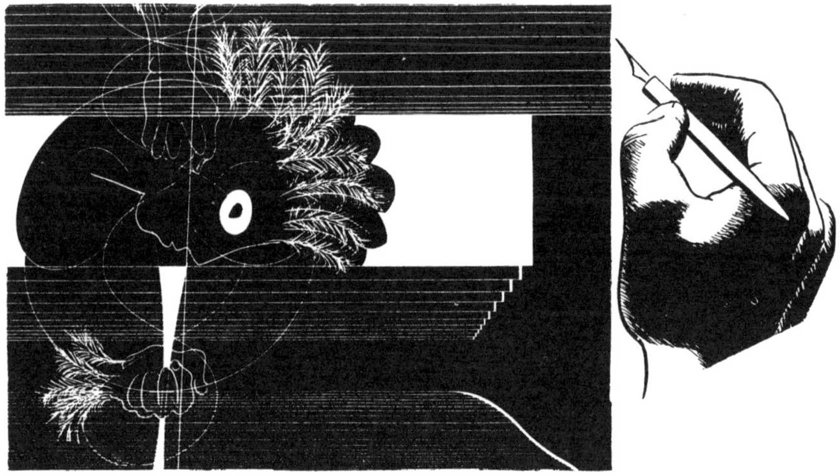

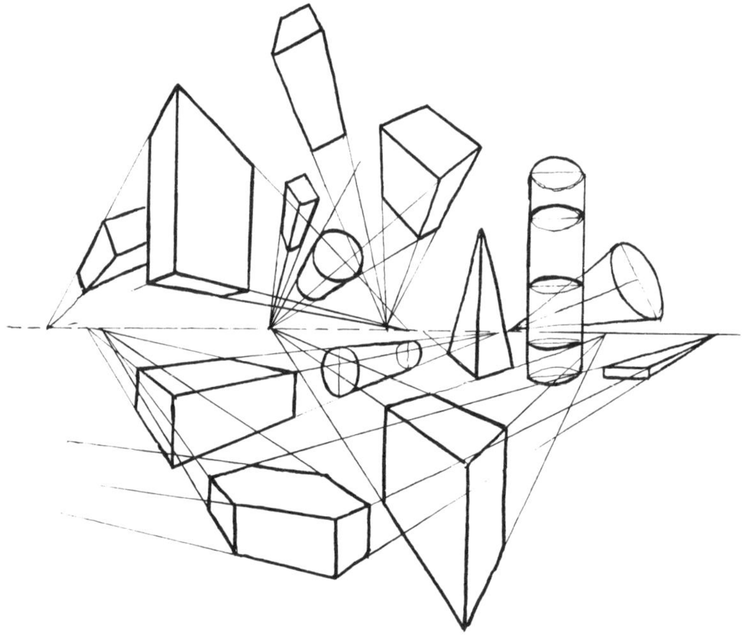

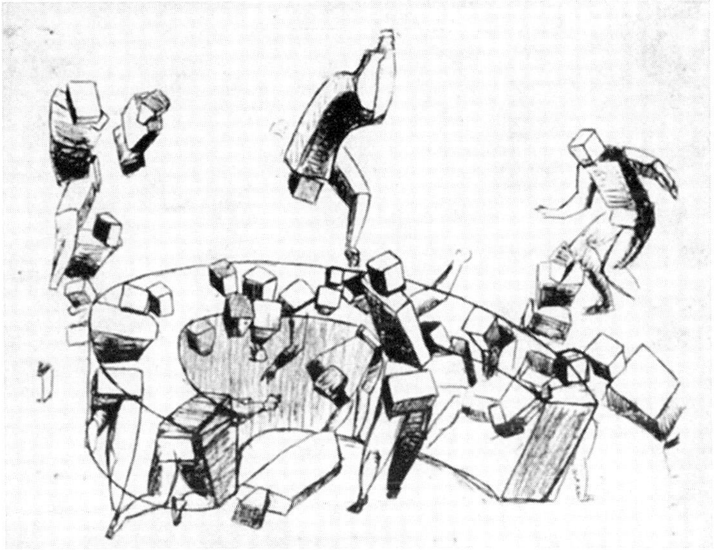

An analysis of the cubical or volume structure of the Tintoretto painting.

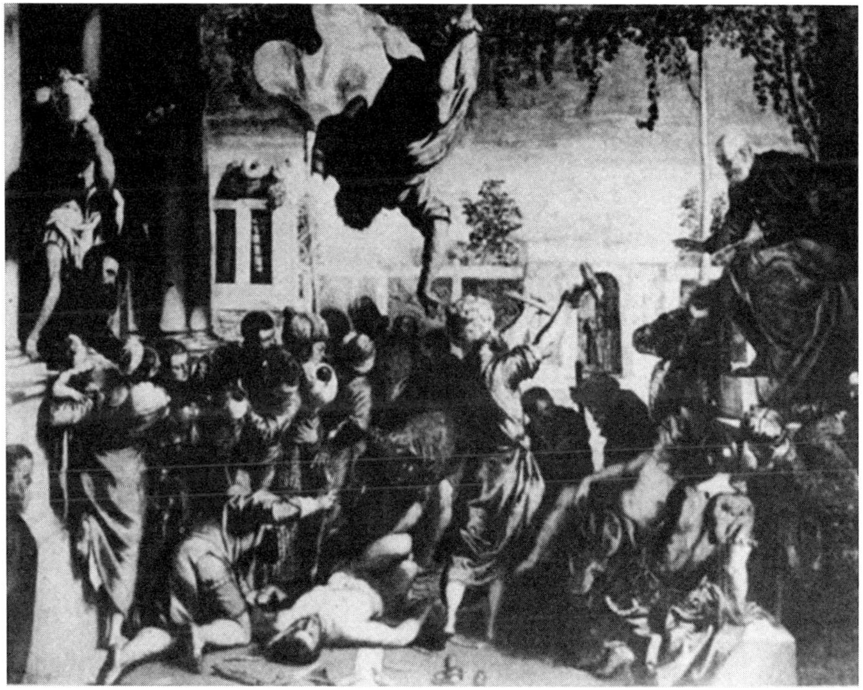

TINTORETTO.
Miracle of St. Mark.
Academy, Venice.

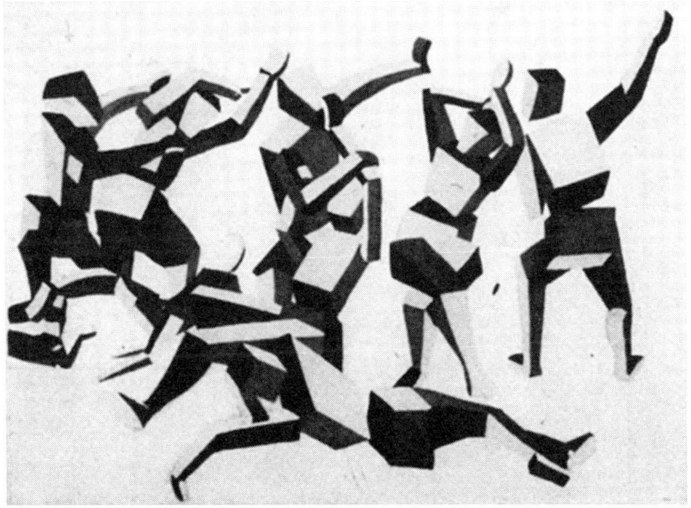

An analysis of the volume movement in a Rubens painting.

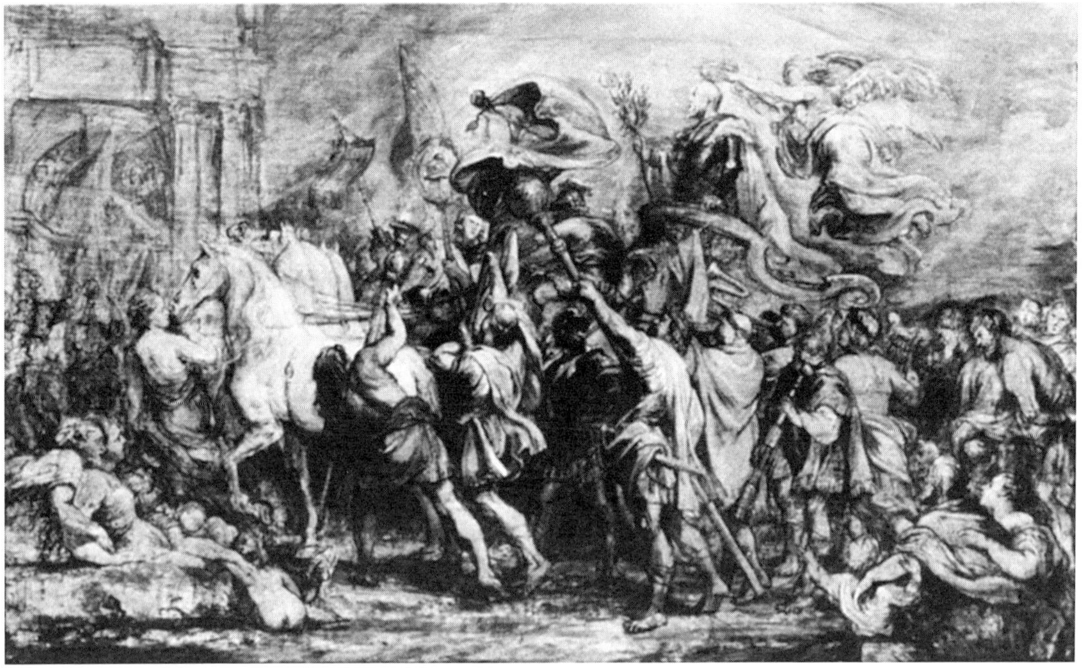

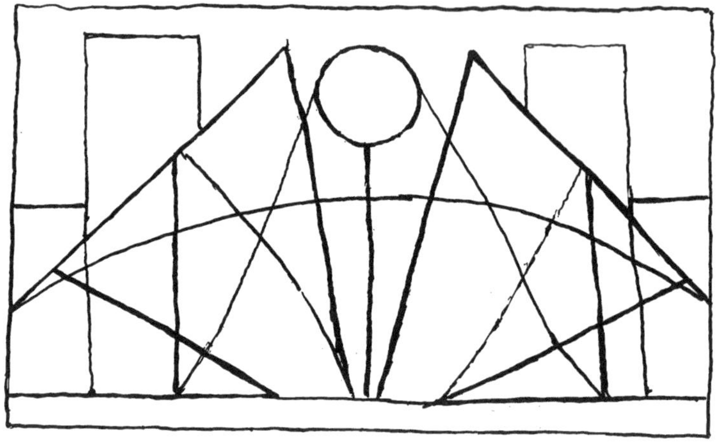

RUBENS.
The Triumphal Entry of Henry IV into Paris.
Metropolitan Museum of Art.

The Rubens painting is based on a geometric and deep space concept.

The etching by Vincent Malta is flat or two-dimensional in its design.

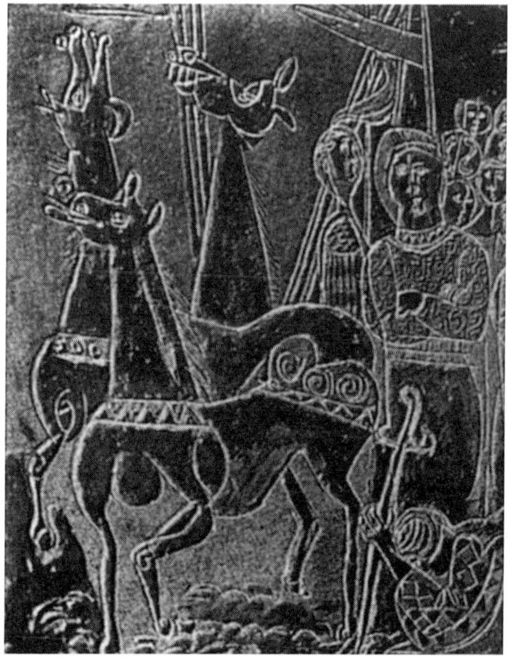

V. MALTA.
Aquatint.
Courtesy of the Artist.

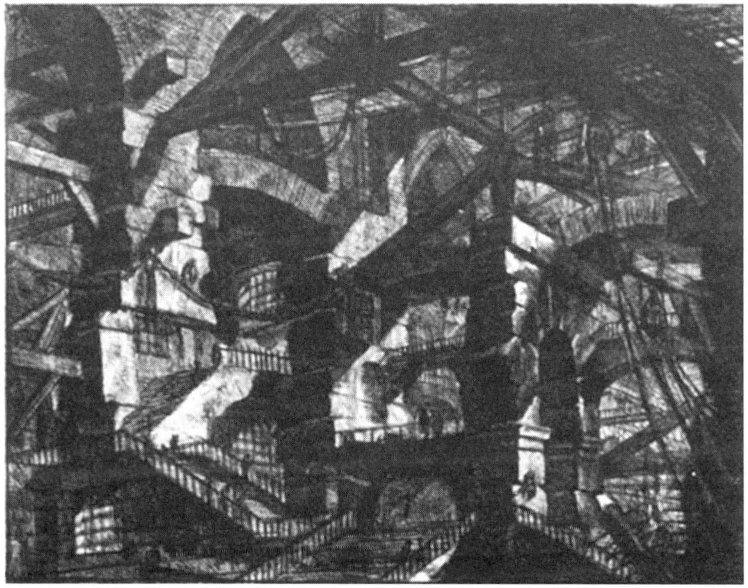

G. B. PIRANESI.
Prison Scene.
Philadelphia Museum of Art.

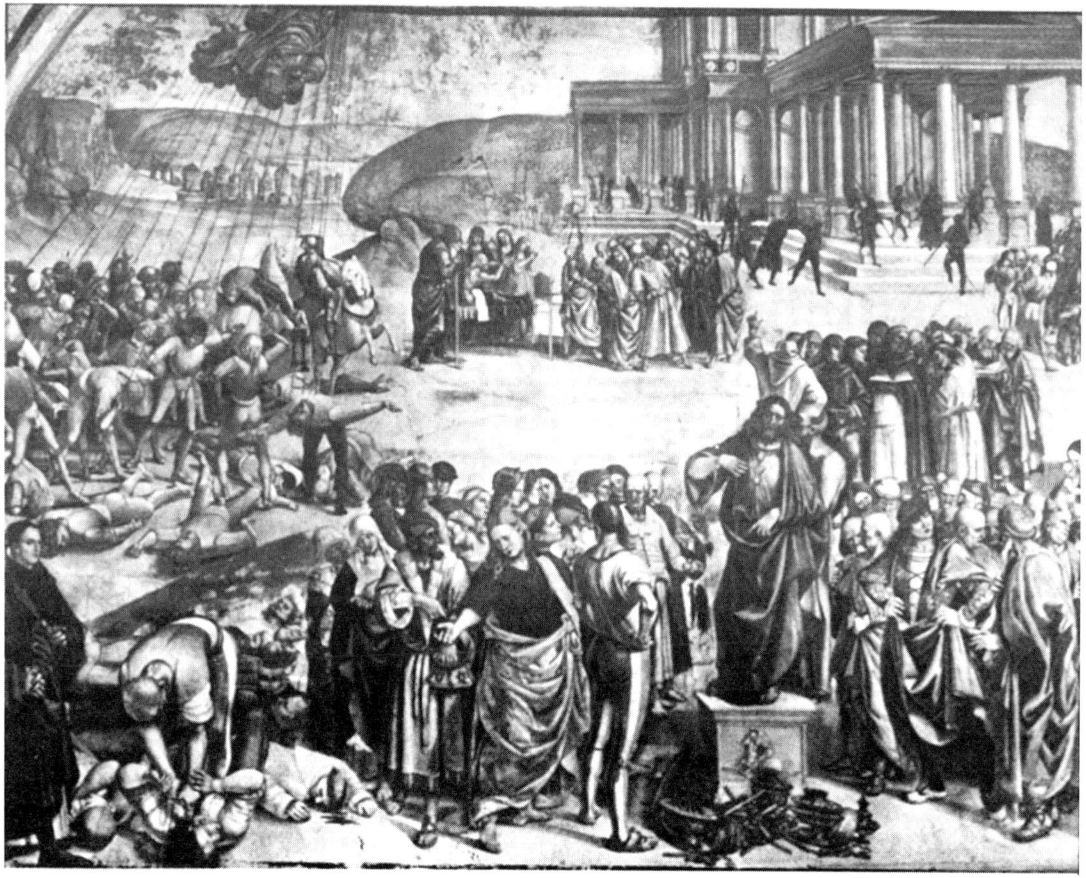

SIGNORELLI.
Detail.
Metropolitan Museum of Art.

EXERCISE

The two pictures above, among others in this book, should be used by the student for analysis of geometric structure. Choose other examples and see if you can find their geometric pattern.

The following chapter on analyzing pictures deals with methods of analysis in greater detail.

ANALYZING PICTURES

Analysis serves as a means of design dissection to bare the underlying structural elements in a picture.

When looking at a picture, we experience a complex set of visual experiences. The story, the symbols, the details, all the elements of the picture, interfere with seeing the design structure. These distractive elements must be pushed aside in order to observe the structure beneath. This can be accomplished by analysis.

All literary detail must be eliminated. Each object in the picture is then reduced to a basic shape. It is only then that the structural skeleton of the design can be seen. In this chapter various analytical means are discussed and demonstrated.

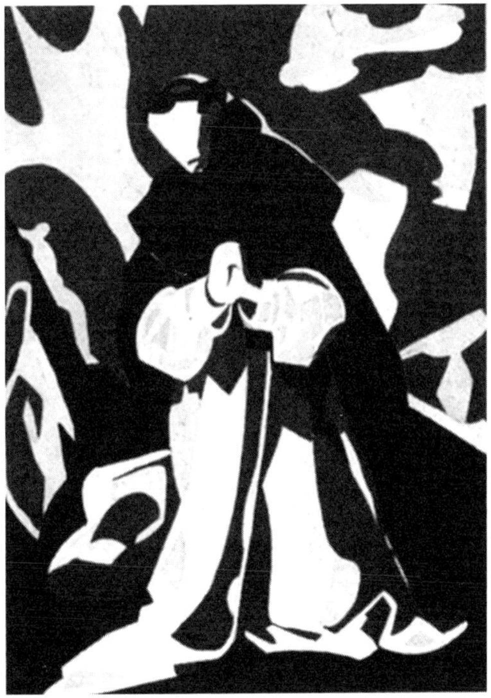

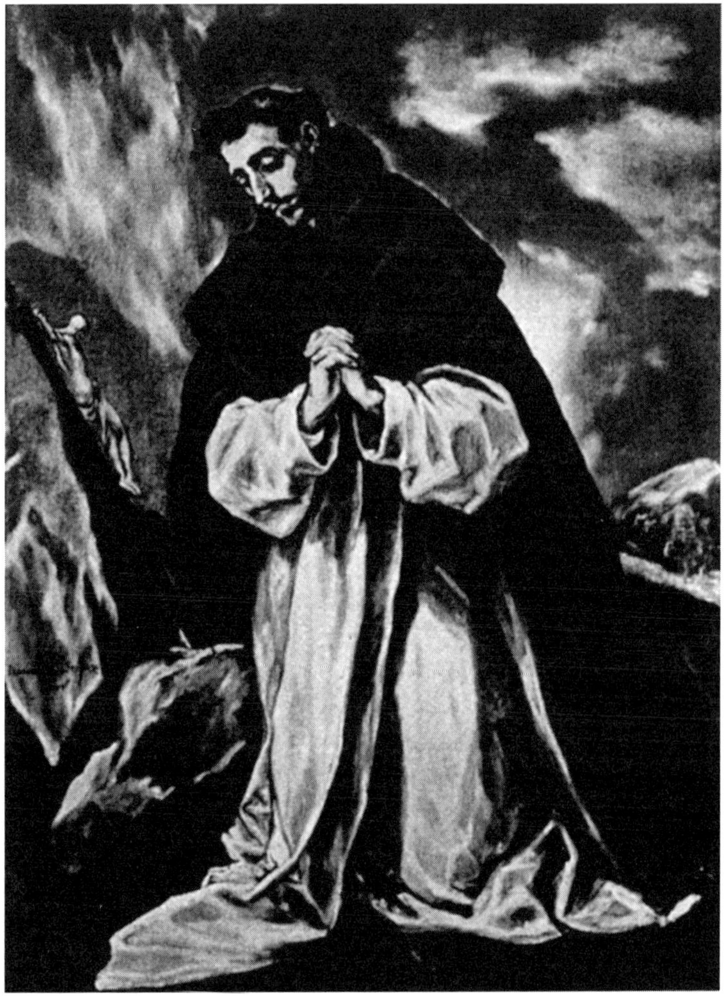

EL GRECO.
Kneeling Saint.

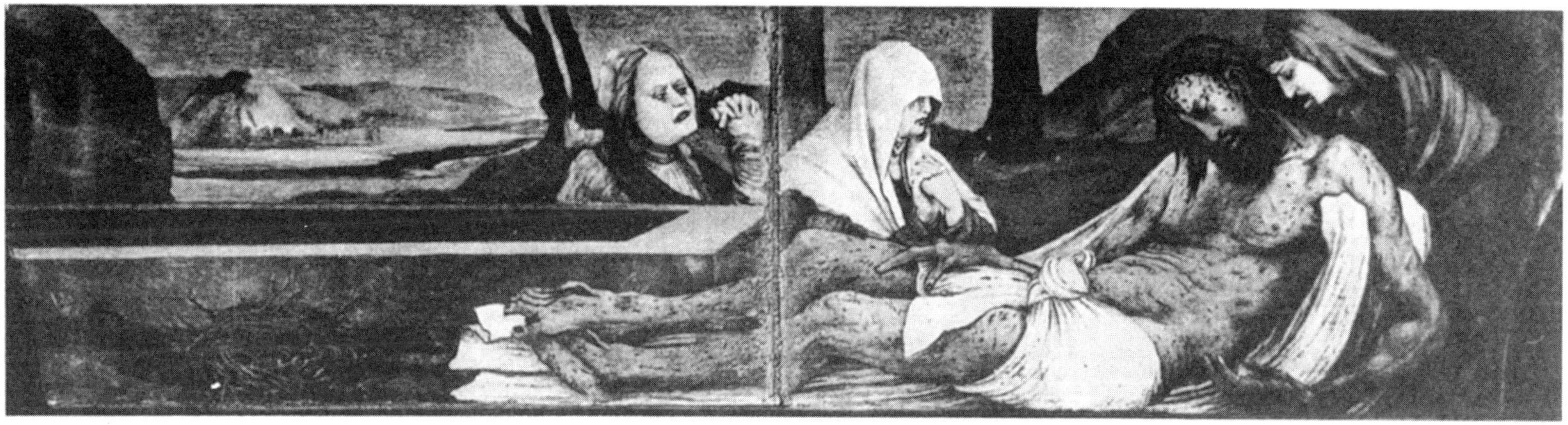

GRUNEWALD.
Altar Triptych.
Photo Courtesy of Metropolitan Museum of Art.

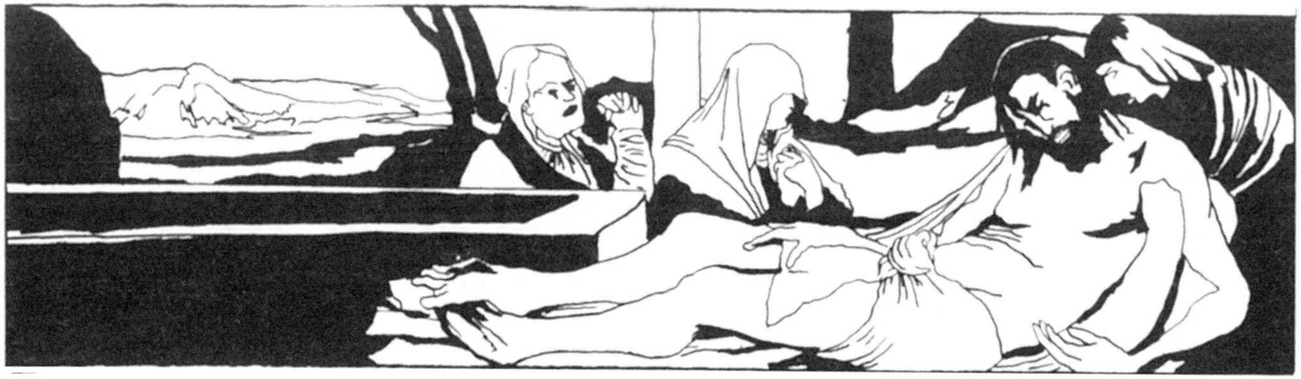

Analysis of Blacks.

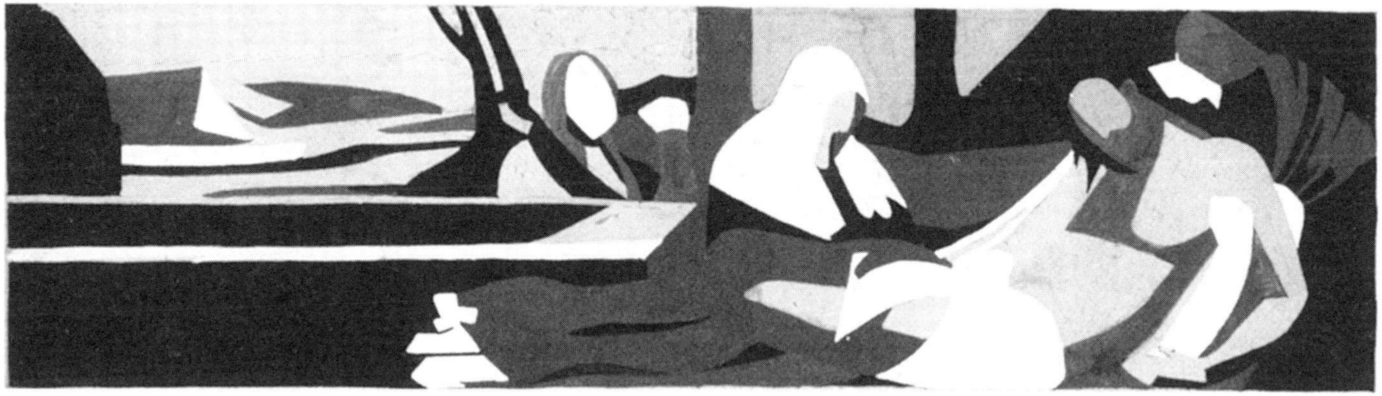

Analysis of Blacks, Whites and Grays.

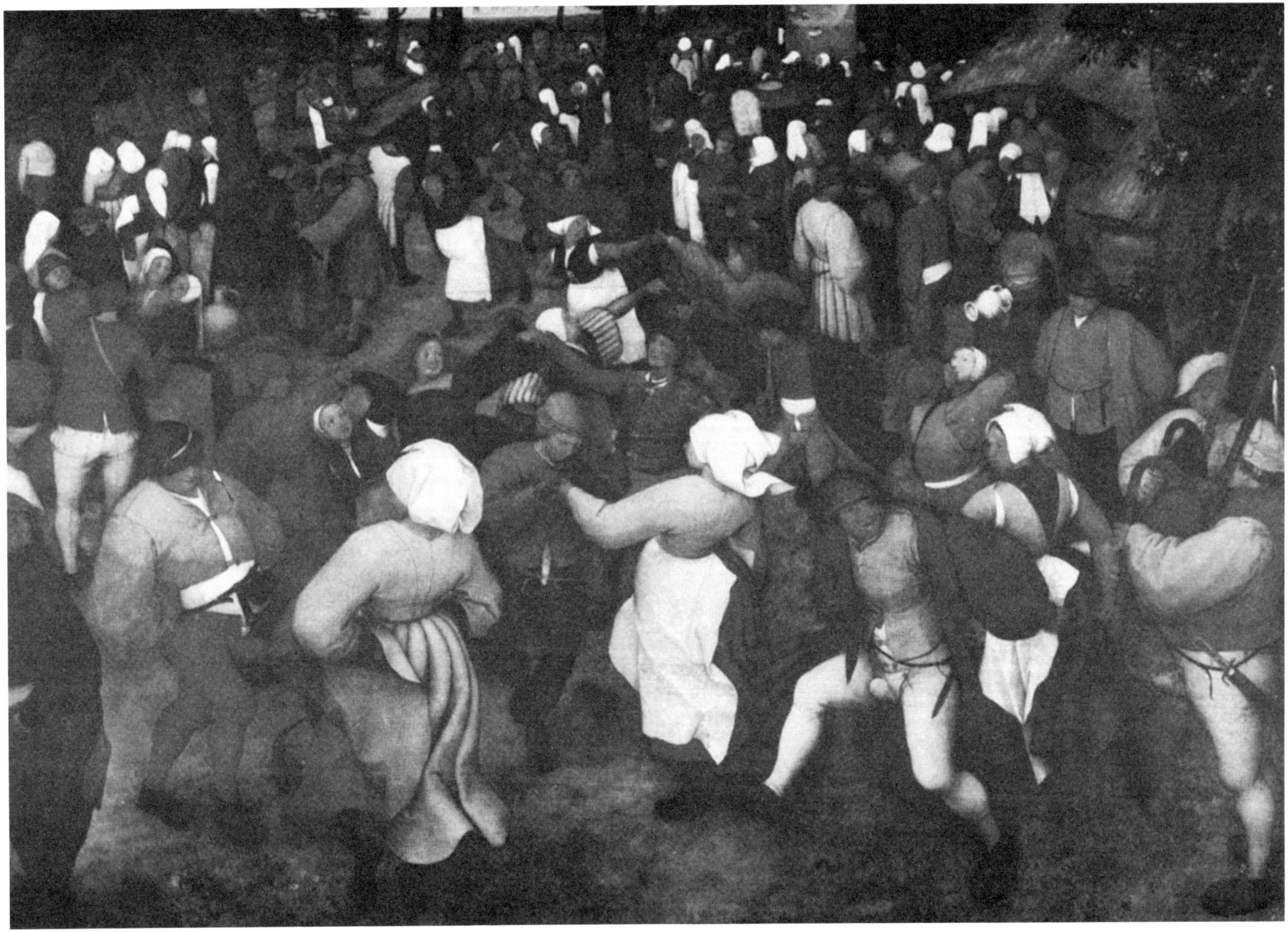

BREUGHEL.
Peasant Dance.

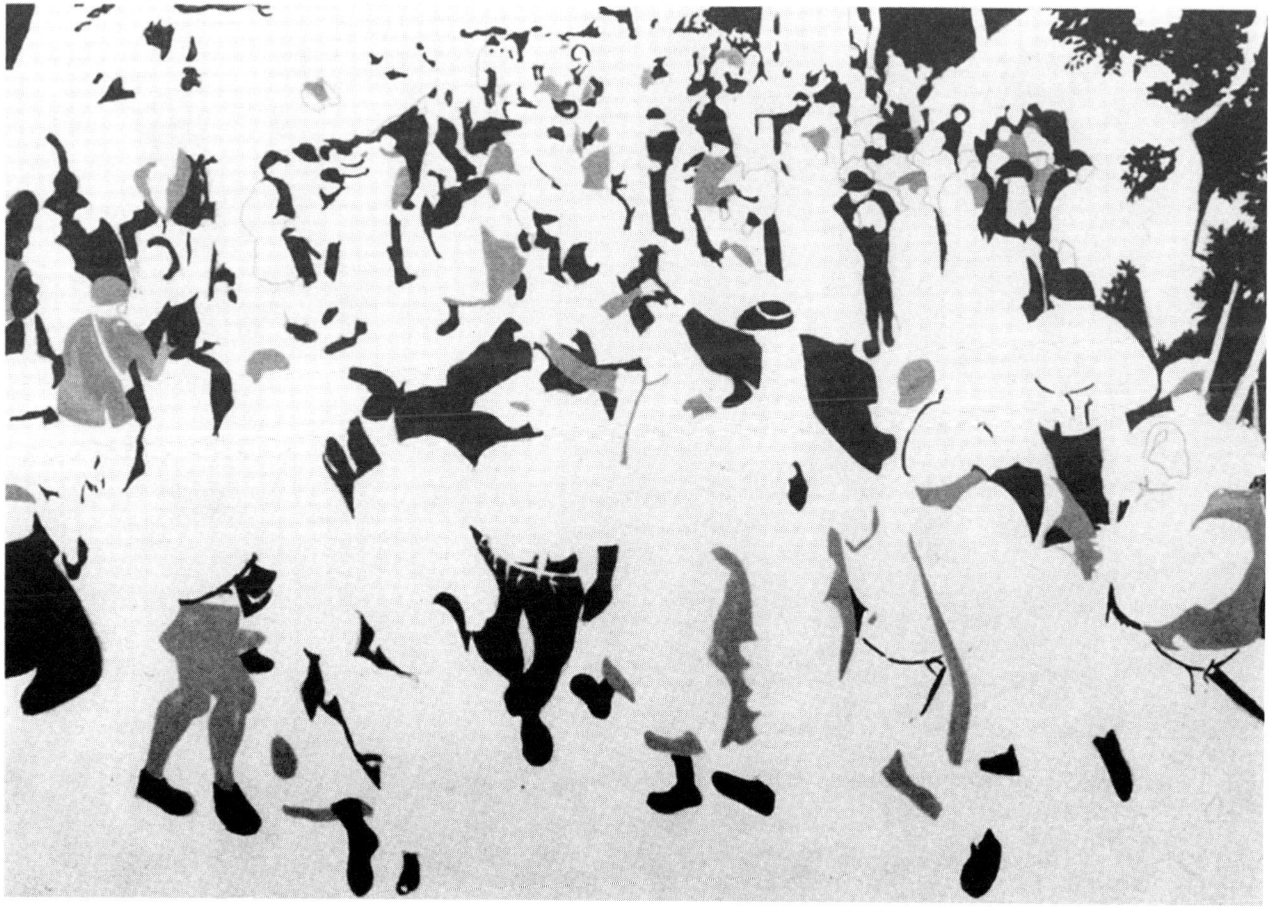

The analysis of the Breughel on the opposite page is particularly interesting because it gives evidence of the beautiful abstract design that underlies the literary communication. Note, in the analysis, the depth of spatial feeling resulting from diminishing the scale of the shapes as they recede. Breughel's inventiveness in varying the size and activity of the shapes in the picture results in an exciting visual experience.

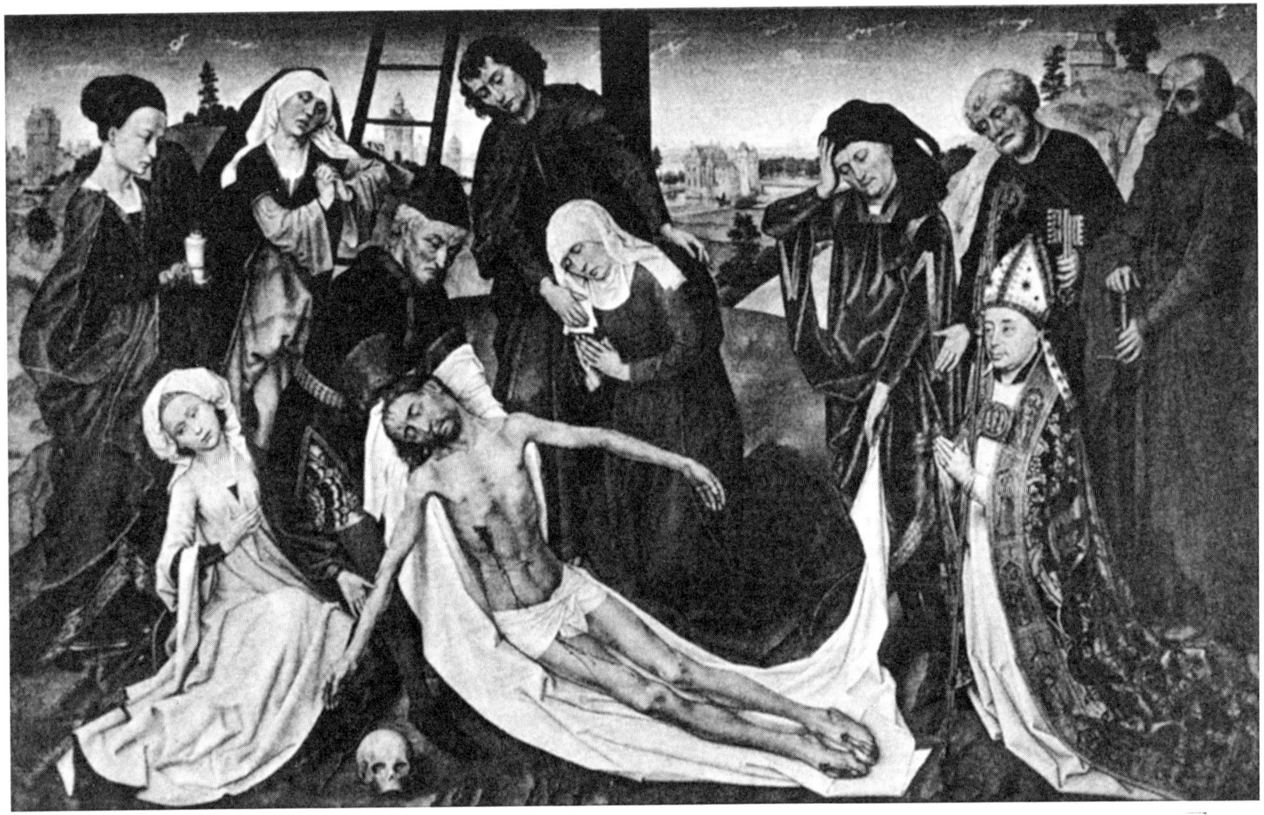

VAN DER WEYDEN.
Pieta.
Photo Courtesy of Metropolitan Museum of Art.

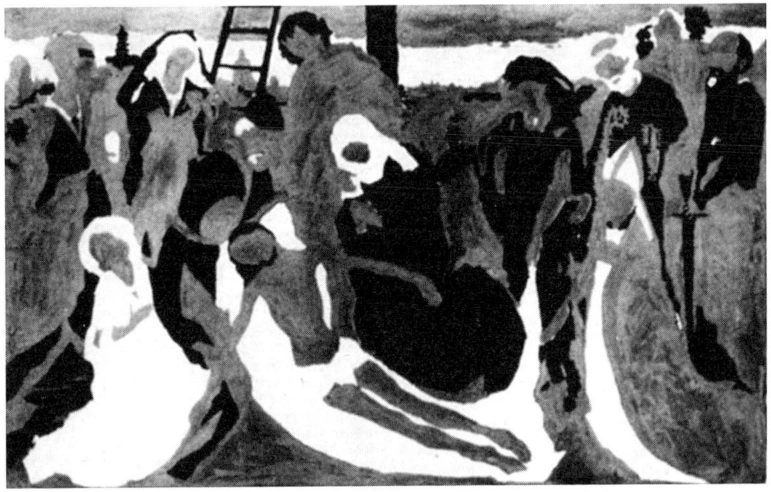

Analysis of Value Patterns.

TINTORETTO.
Miracle of the Loaves and Fishes.
Metropolitan Museum of Art.

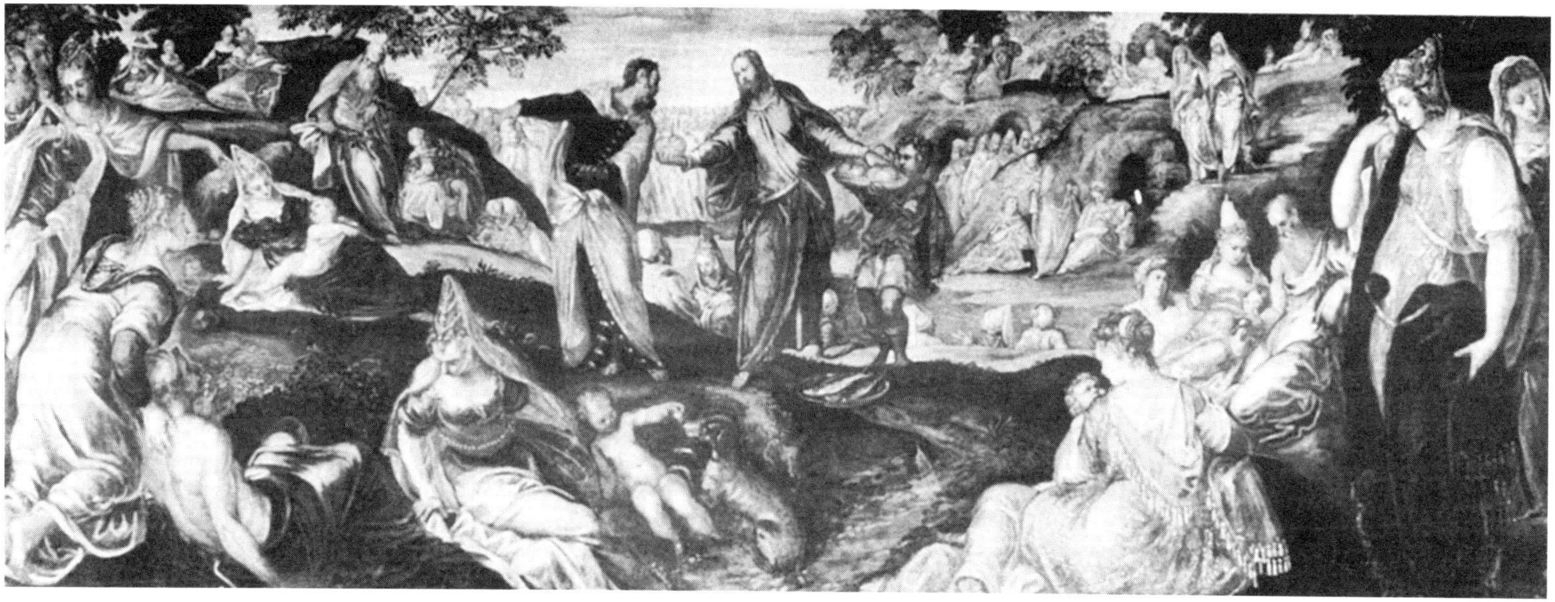

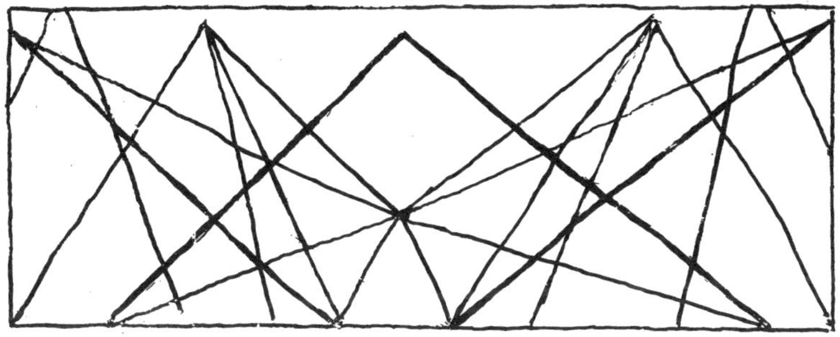

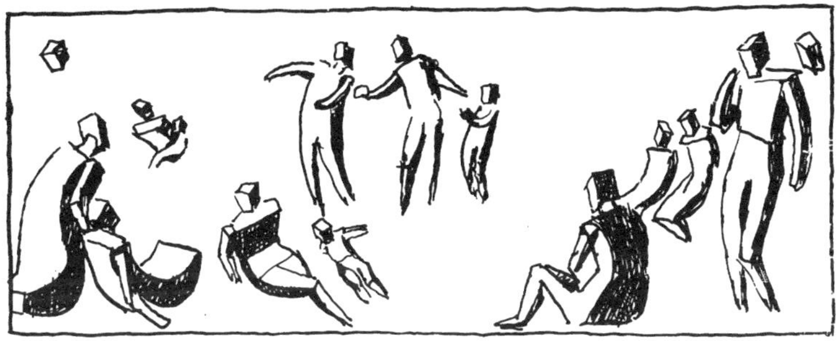

The use of the triangle as a basic design element was common to the Renaissance. The analysis of the Tintoretto at the left makes this quite evident.

The analysis to the right dissects the volume movements of some of the figures.

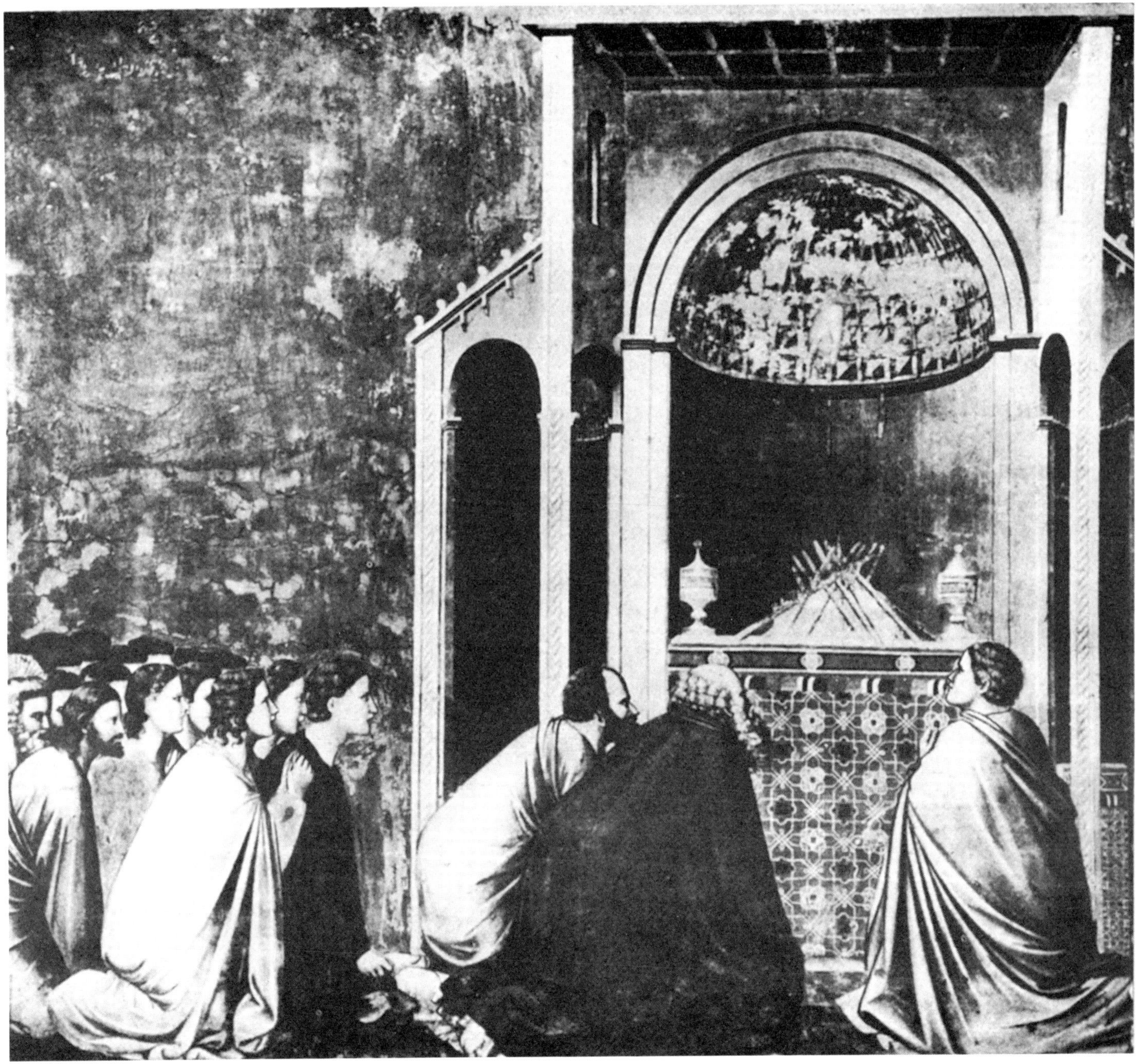

GIOTTO.
Detail.

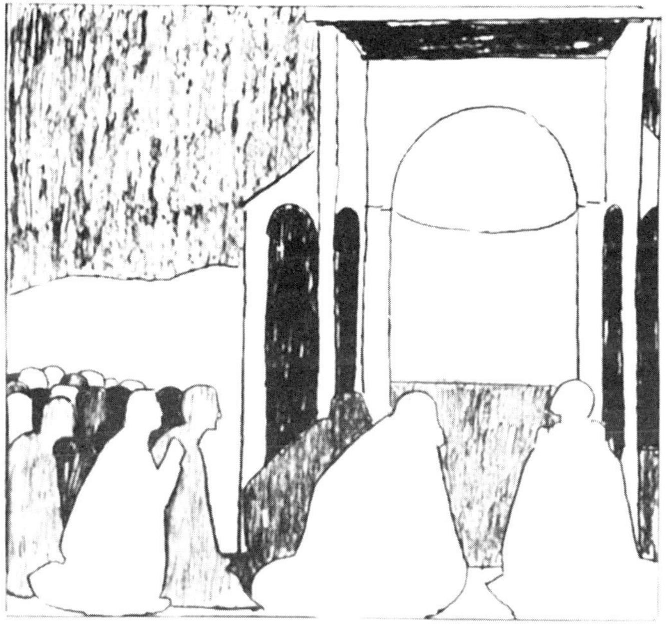

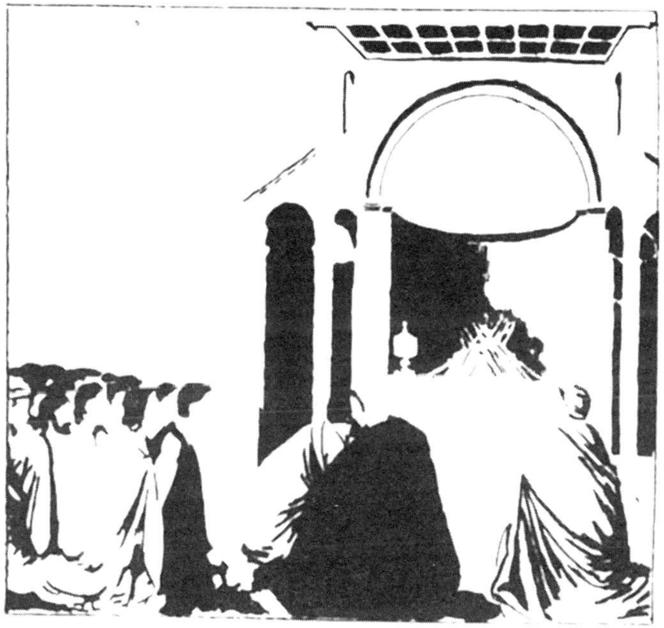

The use of overlapping planes for spatial recession has been discussed in previous chapters. Giotto's use of this principle is demonstrated in the first analysis.

His use of blacks to activate and unify the space is evident in the second analysis.

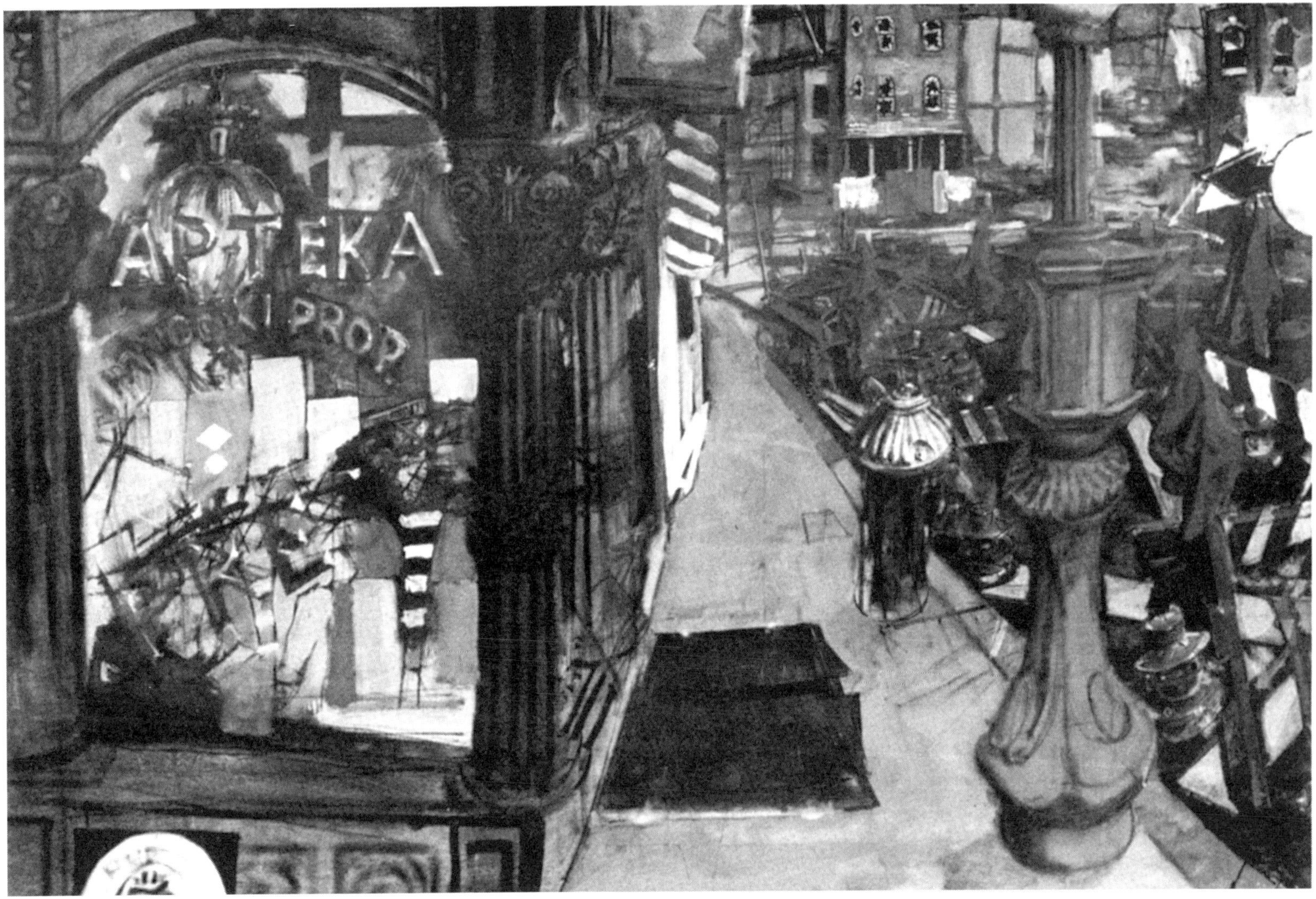

JACK LEVINE.
Apteka.
Collection of Dr. Michael Watter.

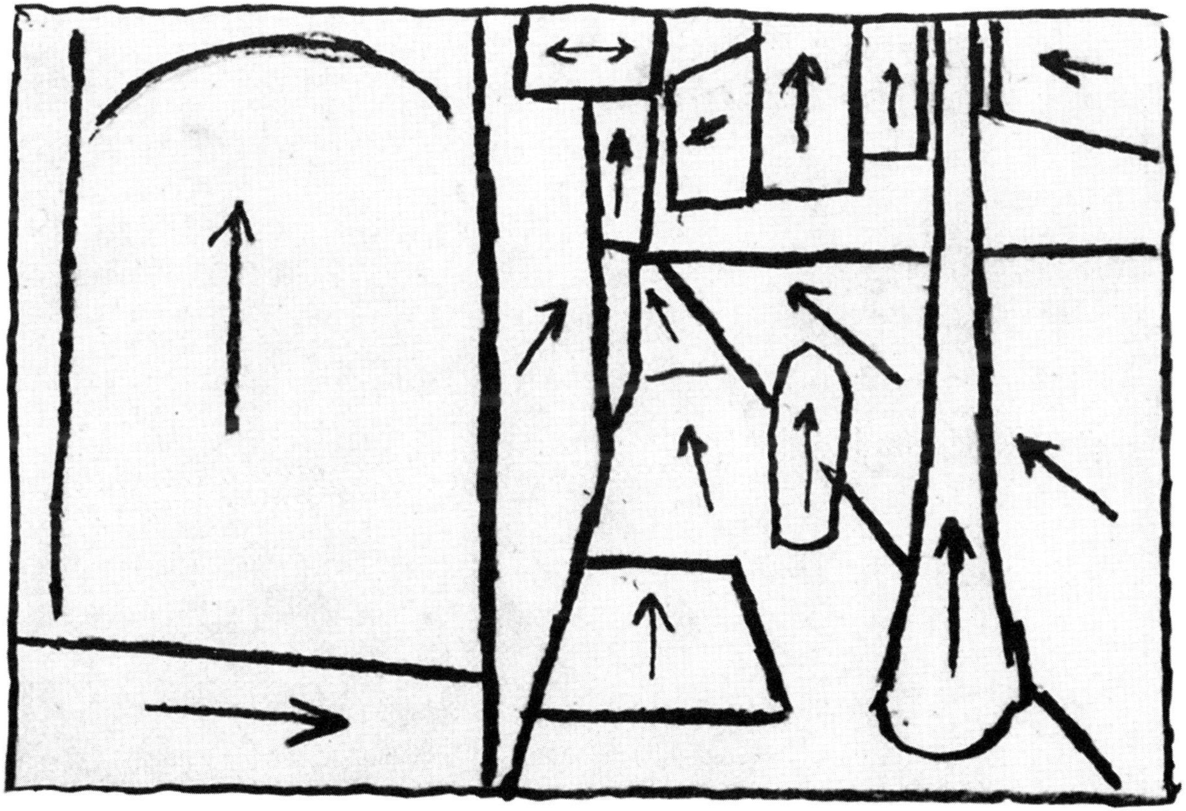

The design of the Levine painting is based on planes tilted into perspective. The planes are arranged so as to move swiftly and recessively, penetrating into deep space. The direction of the planes is indicated by the arrows.

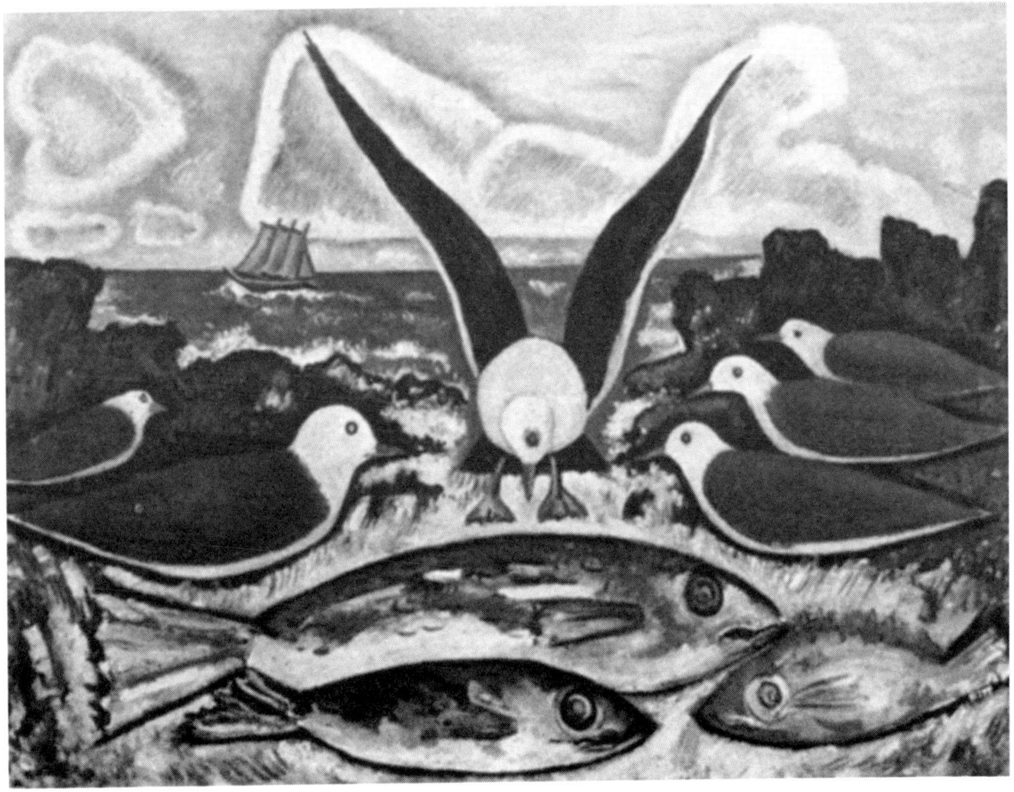

MARSDEN HARTLEY.
Give Us This Day.
Collection of Mr. & Mrs. Hudson Walker.
Photo Courtesy Frick Art Library.

Analysis.

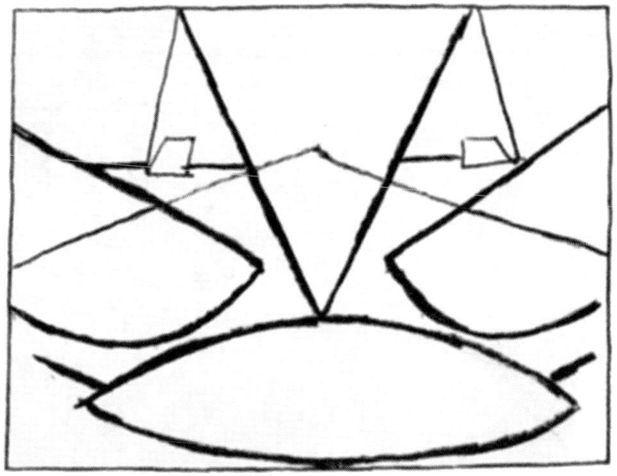

OROZCO
Zapatistas.
Collection Museum of Modern Art.

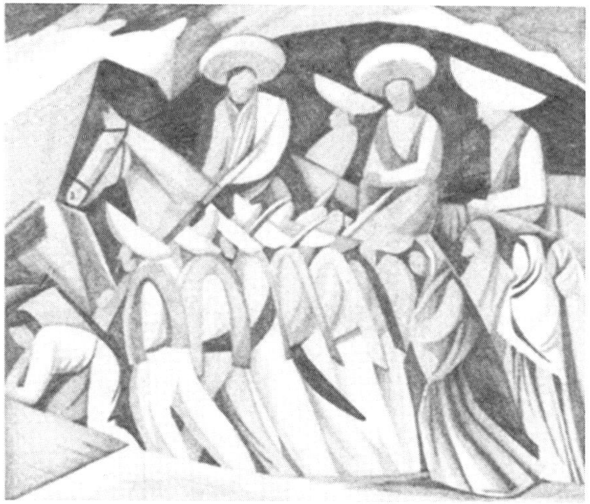

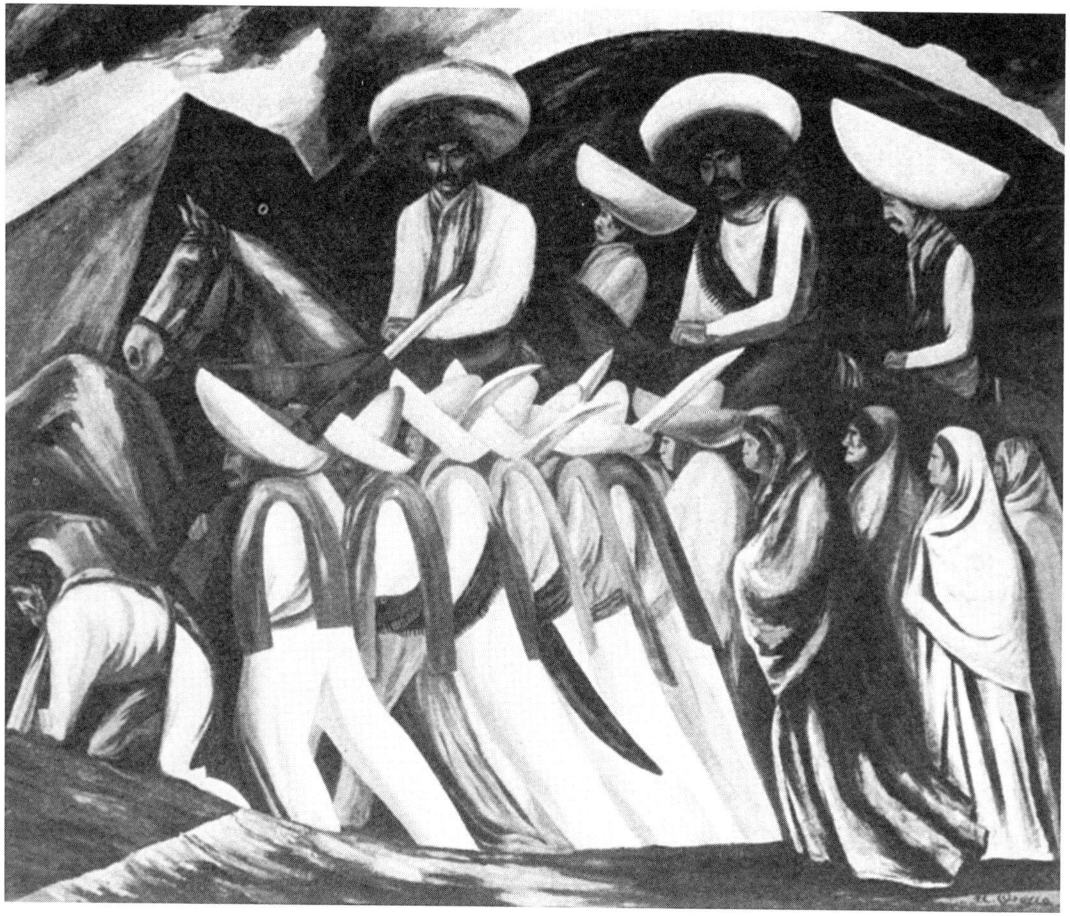

Orozco's picture is dominantly structured with planes in a shallow depth of space. The spatial depth is limited to overlapping planes. The tilt of the planes to the left serves to communicate the sensation of marching. The use of sharply contrasting blacks and whites adds an air of drama to the picture.

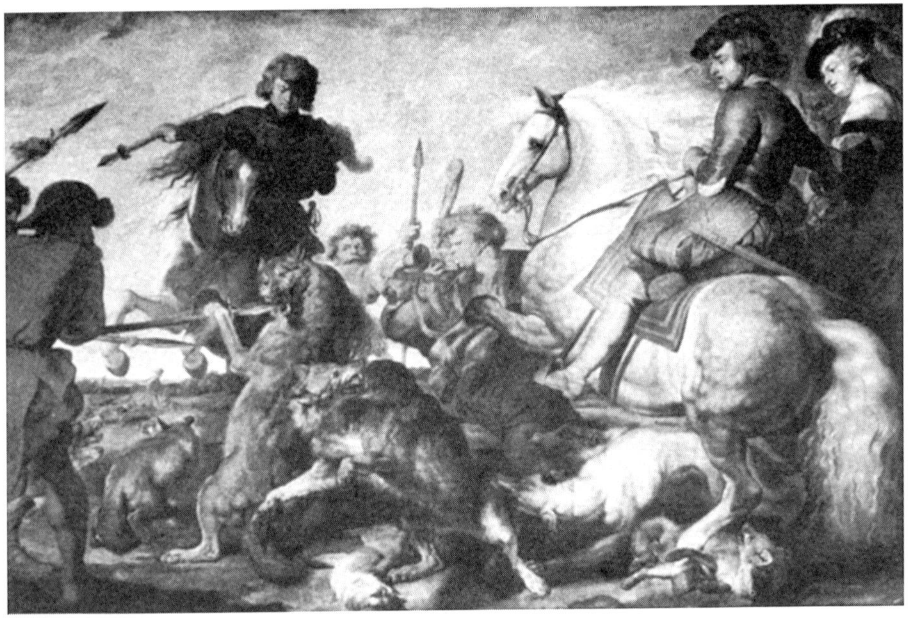

RUBENS.
Wolf and Fox Hunt.
Metropolitan Museum of Art.

The two pictures on this page and the Cézanne on the opposite page are presented for analytical study by the reader.

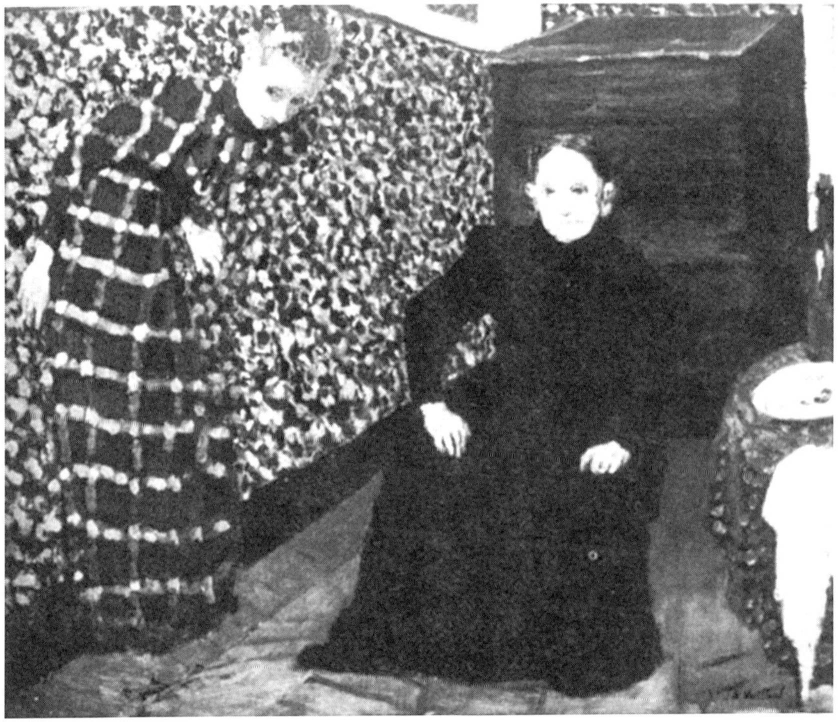

J. VUILLARD.
Mother and Sister of the Artist.
Collection Museum of Modern Art.

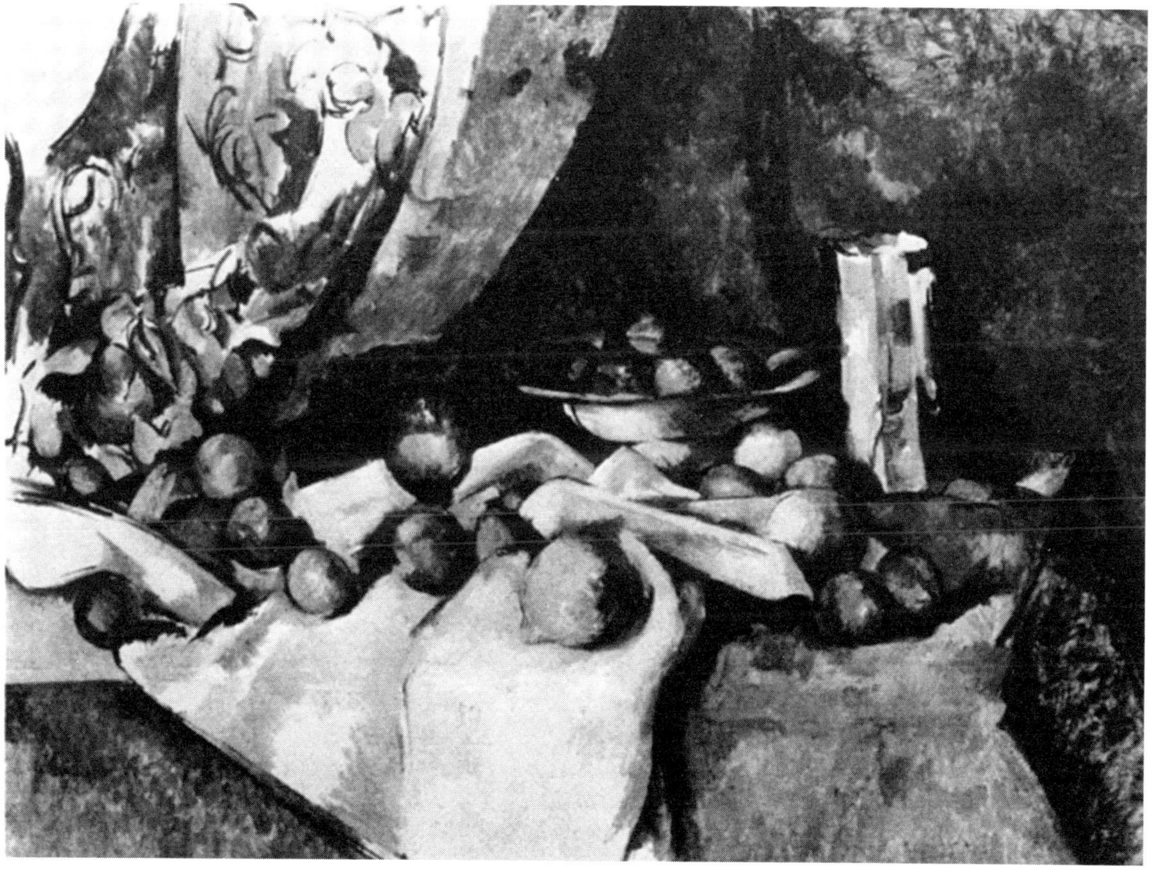

CEZANNE.
Still Life with Apples.
Collection Museum of Modern Art.

EXERCISE

Various principles of composition and methods of analysis have been developed in this book. With sheets of acetate or tracing paper and black lithograph pencil or ink, and with the wealth of reproductions available, an exciting field of learning can be opened for exploration and study.

No other exercise can better develop an understanding of design, nor better inform on the structural principles of picture making, than intensive and thorough analysis of the masters.

This book is dedicated to my wife Mary.

ACKNOWLEDGEMENTS

I should like to express my thanks to the directors of the museums and art galleries who assisted me in assembling the material for this book.

The photographers who took the pictures are: Oliver Baker, Colten, Bruce Elkus, Walter Rosenblum, Soichi Sunami, Elizabeth Timberman.

The exercises and student problems reproduced are by my students at the Art Students League of New York.